Cross Stitch
Cards
100

Joanne Sanderson

D&C
David and Charles
www.mycraftivity.com

This book is for Jeremy and Rianna

A DAVID & CHARLES BOOK
Copyright © David & Charles Limited 2009

David & Charles is an F+W Media Inc. company
4700 East Galbraith Road
Cincinnati, OH 45236

First published in the UK and US in 2009

Text and designs copyright © Joanne Sanderson 2009
Layout and photography copyright © David & Charles 2009

A catalogue record for this book is available from the British Library.

ISBN 13: 978-0-7153-3013-5 hardback
ISBN 10: 0-7153-3013-6
ISBN 13: 978-0-7153-3014-2 paperback
ISBN 10: 0-7153-3014-4

Printed in China by Shenzhen Donnelley
Printing Co. Ltd. for David & Charles
Brunel House, Newton Abbot, Devon

Senior Commissioning Editor: Cheryl Brown
Editor: Bethany Dymond
Assistant Editor: Kate Nicholson
Project Editor and Chart Preparation: Lin Clements
Designer: Mia Farrant
Production Controller: Ros Napper
Photographer: Kim Sayer

Visit our website at www.davidandcharles.co.uk

David & Charles books are available from all good bookshops; alternatively you can contact our Orderline on 0870 9908222 or write to us at FREEPOST EX2 110, D&C Direct, Newton Abbot, TQ12 4ZZ (no stamp required UK only); US customers call 800-289-0963 and Canadian customers call 800-840-5220.

Contents

Introduction

Stitching and giving a hand-made card is a real pleasure, and there are 100 wonderful cross stitch motifs in this book to suit all of the important occasions in life – perfect keepsakes for all of your family and friends. The cross stitch designs are easy to stitch and a major feature of the cards is the attractive decoration and embellishments that have been added to them. I will show you how easy it is to finish off your cards professionally with a range of papercrafting embellishments and simple techniques.

The card designs are spread throughout 11 chapters, making it easy for you to select the right card for the right occasion. Throughout most of the chapters you will also find alphabets and numerals charted, to allow you to personalize the designs by changing ages and adding names and other messages.

Baby Cards features a range of delicious designs perfect to celebrate this joyous event, with colour schemes for baby boys, baby girls and twins.

Cards for Girls has fabulous cards for girls from toddlers to teenagers and the cards are easily personalized and adapted to send good luck wishes and congratulations.

Cards for Boys shows how to create fun cards for boys of all ages and some of the designs can be used for congratulations and good luck as well as birthdays.

Cards for Women focuses on delightful cards to send love and support to all the women that are important to us.

Cards for Men has some great cards for some of the wonderful men in our lives, including the themes of sports, racing cars, gardening and football.

People with Passions is filled with cards suitable for popular passions, including music, gardening, DIY, cooking, pets and shopping.

Love and Romance has some gorgeous cards celebrating all those lovey-dovey occasions, including Valentine's Day, engagements, weddings and anniversaries.

New Horizons provides you with card ideas to celebrate memorable events and great achievements, such as graduating, passing a driving test and emigrating.

Calendar Events has attractive designs to celebrate seasonal events through the year – from Easter and St Patrick's Day to Hallowe'en and Thanksgiving.

Cards for Christmas has some colourful festive cards, both contemporary and traditional, which will stand out from shop-bought greetings.

Last-minute Greetings features 20 quick-to-stitch cards and tags for those unexpected occasions or events, allowing you to create lovely designs even when time is short.

Overleaf you will find the Quick Stitch section, which gives all the stitching advice you need to get you started. After you have stitched your design comes the fun part of decorating and embellishing your card. A design can be simply mounted into an aperture card, but with a little more effort, and a lot more fun, I show you how to combine cross stitch with papercrafting techniques to create some truly memorable cards (see opposite). Hand Crafting Cards (page 7) is a useful preview to the card-making techniques used in the book, and if my card designs have inspired you to create your own, you'll find all the information you need in Making and Finishing Cards (pages 100–103).

One Card – Three Ways

The choice of embellishments today is excitingly wide, but can be a little daunting when you are deciding how to finish off a stitched piece. The cross stitch motifs in the book are very versatile – with a slight change, perhaps in the wording on the card or the embellishments used, a design can be used for more than one occasion. Here I show you three basic ways to finish a card.

1 Mounted in a simple double-fold card with aperture.

2 Mounted as a patch on a single-fold card.

3 Mounted as a patch on a decorated single-fold card with themed embellishments added.

It's your choice as to whether you simply slip your stitched design into an aperture card, or spend a little more time finishing your card to make it extra special. At the back of the book (pages 100–103) you will find a useful section with more detailed advice on card-making and finishing techniques. Just remember, there is no right or wrong way to finish a card, and you can decide just how much or how little you want to do, so feel free to experiment. I hope that the card designs I have included throughout the book will inspire you to create your own.

1 Here a cross stitch design was stitched on white fabric and simply mounted into a double-fold card with an oval aperture – quick and easy.

2 Here the same design was stitched and this time backed with iron-on interfacing to stabilize the fabric edges. It was then trimmed and glued to a single-fold card as an attractive patch.

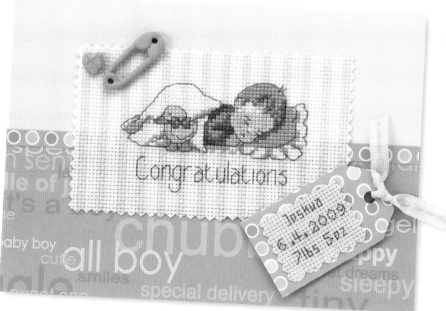

3 Here the design was stitched on patterned fabric and prepared as a patch as before, but the card itself was decorated with printed papers and the cross stitch design teamed with themed embellishments, producing a professional look that is surprisingly easy to achieve.

Quick Stitch

Read this section to get you started. It is very useful for beginners because it contains the basic information you need to stitch the designs, and also gives 12 useful tips for producing lovely stitching. See pages 98–99 for further information on the stitching materials and equipment you will need, detailed stitching techniques and how to work the stitches.

Before starting, check the design size given with each project and make sure that this is the size you require for your finished embroidery. The fabric you are stitching on should be about 7.5–10cm (3–4in) larger all round than the finished stitching, to allow for making up.

Organize your threads before you start a project as this will help to avoid confusion later. Put the threads required for a particular project on an organizer (available from craft shops) and always include the manufacturer's name and the shade number. You can make your own thread organizer by punching holes along one side of a piece of thick card.

When you have cut the length of stranded cotton (floss) you need, usually about 46cm (18in), separate out all the strands before taking the number you need, realigning them and threading your needle.

If using a hoop, avoid placing it over worked stitches as it will squash them, and remove the hoop from the fabric at the end of a stitching session.

If using metallic threads, work with shorter lengths, about 30.5cm (12in), to avoid wear on the thread.

The designs in this book have been stitched over one block of a 14-count Aida, but you could also work over two threads of a 28-count evenweave fabric.

DMC stranded cotton (floss) has been used to stitch the designs, but you could use Anchor or Madeira if you prefer by matching the colours using a colour card, available at craft shops.

Work the cross stitch designs from the centre of the fabric and the centre of the chart outwards.

Unless otherwise stated, stitch the designs with two strands of thread for cross stitch, two strands for French knots wound once around the needle and one strand for backstitch.

For neat cross stitching, work the top stitches so they all face in the same direction.

If your thread begins to twist, turn the work upside down and let the needle spin.

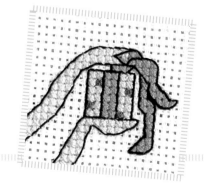

When adding a backstitch outline, add it after the cross stitch has been completed to prevent the solid line of the backstitch being broken.

Hand Crafting Cards

This section is a useful preview of the basic card-making techniques used in this book to give the finished cards that hand-crafted look that makes each one unique for the occasion and the person you are stitching it for. All the techniques are very easy to do, yet create some fabulous effects. The cards can be made up in a number of different ways, and personalizing them to suit each individual recipient is part of the fun. You will find all the information you need to get started in Making and Finishing Cards (pages 100–103), including some useful tips on starting to design your own cards for truly individual greetings. Suppliers for the making-up products are given within the chapters, with contact details on page 104.

Layering, that is adding different elements in layers, not only adds interest but can echo the theme of your card and introduce further colour or contrast.

Choose a colour scheme to reflect the theme of the card or the age of the recipient, e.g., softer colours for a new baby card and brighter colours for a toddler.

Selecting card and embellishment colours similar to the thread colours in the design is a good way to produce harmony.

Choosing an embellishment to complement the theme of a card, and the recipient, is the recipe to success.

Baby Cards

The birth of a new baby is a joyous and often much longed-for occasion and what better way to celebrate the event than with a gorgeous hand-stitched card. New parents will be thrilled with such a gesture and the card can be kept forever as a memento of the birth.

The cards in this chapter are perfect for celebrating important milestones in the life of a new baby, including the announcement of the birth, congratulations to the proud parents and best wishes for a christening or a baby's first birthday. The colour schemes have been chosen so they can be easily changed to suit either a baby boy or baby girl.

Make it special. . .
There are a vast number of baby-themed embellishments available in pretty, sugary shades and a selection is shown here. Cards for newborns are often soft and gentle, much like the baby, so choose soft pastels and neutral colours for embellishments to balance with the cross stitch designs.

Baby Boy Announcement

The printed Aida used for this sweet card adds an extra dimension to the charming design.

Stitch count 25h x 51w
Design size 4.5 x 9.3cm (1⅞ x 3¾in)

You will need

15 x 20cm (6 x 8in) 14-count printed Aida (DMC DC27C bleu) ★
Size 26 tapestry needle ★
DMC threads as listed in chart key ★

For the stitching, use two strands for full and three-quarter cross stitch and one strand for French knots and for backstitch. See pages 98–99 if necessary.

To finish, mount the stitching in a double-fold card with an oval aperture. Glue a strip of patterned paper 3.5cm (1⅜in) wide to the front base and apply baby-themed embellishments and stickers to each side of the aperture.

Baby Girl Announcement

All pretty in pink – what an adorable card this is and surely destined to become a treasured keepsake.

Stitch count 24h x 52w
Design size 4.3 x 9.3cm (1¾ x 3¾in)

You will need

★ 15 x 20cm (6 x 8in) 14-count printed Aida (DMC DC27B rose)
★ Size 26 tapestry needle
★ DMC threads as listed in chart key

For the stitching, use two strands for full and three-quarter cross stitch and one strand for French knots and for backstitch. See pages 98–99 if necessary.

To finish, mount the stitching on a pink single-fold card. Add pink and white floral paper to the mount and embellish with with little pink brads and a narrow ribbon bow.

Twins Announcement

This sunny announcement of the birth of twins, simply mounted on yellow gingham, makes the cutest card.

Stitch count 37h x 32w
Design size 6.7 x 5.8cm (2¾ x 2¼in)

You will need

15 x 15cm (6 x 6in) 14-count white Aida ★
Size 26 tapestry needle ★
DMC threads as listed in chart key ★

For the stitching, use two strands for full and three-quarter cross stitch and one strand for French knots and for backstitch. See pages 98–99 if necessary.

To finish, mount the stitching on a single-fold embossed square card (DCWV, see Suppliers). Add yellow gingham patterned paper to the mount, with a single brad as a pram detail.

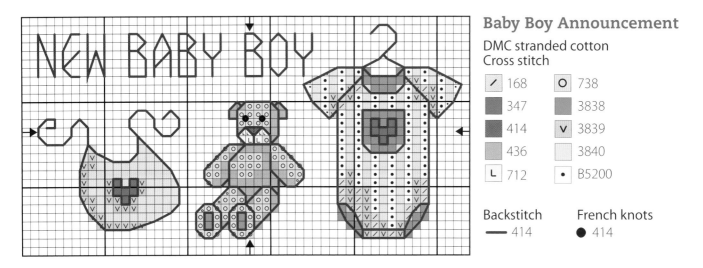

Baby Boy Announcement

DMC stranded cotton
Cross stitch

/	168	O	738
	347		3838
	414	V	3839
	436		3840
L	712	•	B5200

Backstitch
— 414

French knots
● 414

Baby Girl Announcement

DMC stranded cotton
Cross stitch

	151
\	818
	3350
T	3733
•	B5200

Backstitch
— 414

French knots
● 414

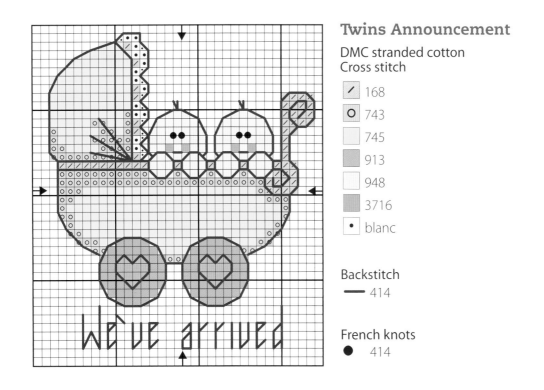

Twins Announcement

DMC stranded cotton
Cross stitch

/	168
O	743
	745
	913
	948
	3716
•	blanc

Backstitch
— 414

French knots
● 414

Welcome Baby Girl

This fun card has been designed for a baby girl but you could change the blanket colour to blue for a boy if desired. A stitched tag contains the baby's name and date of birth.

Stitch count 37h x 46w (for main design)
Design size 6.7 x 8.3cm (2¾ x 3¼in)

You will need

16 x 16cm (6¼ x 6¼in) 14-count pale blue ★
Aida (DMC 800)
7 x 6cm (2¾ x 2⅜in)14-count white Aida for tag ★
Size 26 tapestry needle ★
DMC threads as listed in chart key ★

For the stitching, use two strands for full and three-quarter cross stitch and one strand for backstitch. See pages 98–99 if necessary. Stitch the tag using the alphabet and numbers opposite and add a double border in pink cross stitch.

To finish, trim the fabric with pinking shears. Cover the bottom half of a lemon single-fold card with patterned paper and stick the fabric patch on top using double-sided tape. Cut a tag shape from striped paper and attach the stitched name and date and a ribbon bow. Place baby stickers (Dovecraft) at the bottom of the tag.

Congratulations Baby Boy

A simple stitched tag recording the date and weight of a baby boy personalizes this sweet congratulations card.

Stitch count 30h x 51w (for main design)
Design size 5.4 x 9.2cm (2⅛ x 3¾in)

You will need

★ 16 x 21cm (6¼ x 8¼in) 14-count patterned Aida (DMC DC27R bleu)
★ 6 x 10cm (2½ x 4in) 14-count blue Aida for tag
★ Size 26 tapestry needle
★ DMC threads as listed in chart key

For the stitching, use two strands for cross stitch and one strand for the French knot and for backstitch. See pages 98–99 if necessary. Stitch the tag using the alphabet and numbers charted opposite.

To finish, trim the fabric edges with pinking shears. Glue an 8cm (3in) strip of patterned paper across the front of a lemon single-fold card and stick a 1cm (⅜in) strip of paper across the top edge of the patterned paper. Stick the fabric centrally on the front of the card using double-sided tape. Attach a brad and baby napkin pin embellishment (Dovecraft) to the top left corner of the fabric.

Cut a tag shape from patterned paper and stick the pinked stitched text on top. Add a ribbon bow before sticking the tag on the bottom right corner of the card.

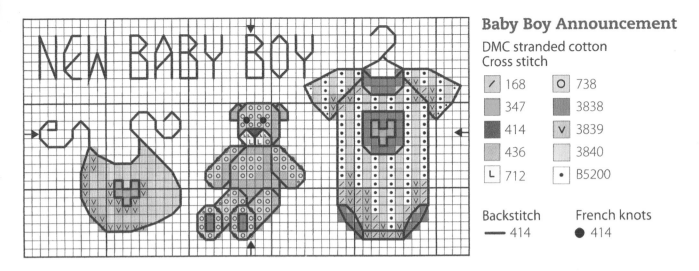

Baby Boy Announcement

DMC stranded cotton
Cross stitch

⁄	168	O	738
	347		3838
	414	V	3839
	436		3840
L	712	•	B5200

Backstitch   French knots
—— 414   ● 414

Baby Girl Announcement

DMC stranded cotton
Cross stitch

	151
⟍	818
	3350
T	3733
•	B5200

Backstitch
—— 414

French knots
● 414

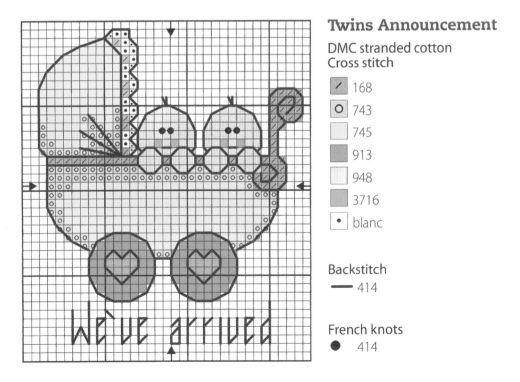

Twins Announcement

DMC stranded cotton
Cross stitch

⁄	168
O	743
	745
	913
	948
	3716
•	blanc

Backstitch
—— 414

French knots
● 414

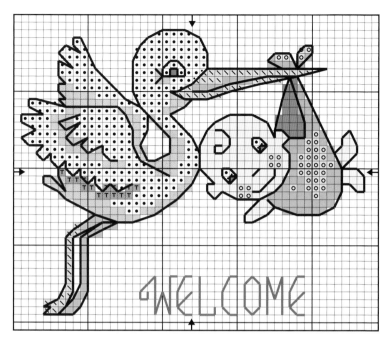

Welcome Baby Girl

DMC stranded cotton
Cross stitch

168	\ 744	3354	• B5200
T 318	948	3731	
742	O 963	3838	

Backstitch
— 150
— 413

Cross stitch   Backstitch
3354   — 414

Use the backstitch alphabet and numerals above to create your own tags or customize the cards in the book. You could change the colours to others of your choice

Congratulations Baby Boy

DMC stranded cotton
Cross stitch

T 168	L 738	745	3839
\ 353	741	948	O 3840
V 436	/ 743	▬ 3838	• B5200

Backstitch
— 414

French knot
● 414

Christening

Delicate colours and seed beads add a vintage effect to this traditional christening card. Designed to give a timeless elegance to this special occasion, it is suitable for a baby boy or girl.

Stitch count 28h x 22w (maximum for each motif)
Design size 5 x 4cm (2 x 1½in) (maximum)

You will need
★ Three 12 x 10cm (4¾ x 4in) pieces of 14-count mint green Aida (DMC 964)
★ Size 26 tapestry needle
★ DMC threads as listed in chart key
★ Cream seed beads

For the stitching, use two strands for cross stitch and one strand for backstitch. See pages 98–99 if necessary. Attach the beads (see page 99) in the positions shown on the chart.

To finish, trim the fabric with pinking shears. Stick a 5cm (2in) wide strip of yellow card across the front of a single-fold card, concealing the edge with ribbon. Stick the stitched pieces to the front of the card with double-sided tape. Attach a banner (Ali Craft) and adhesive stones (Papermania).

1st Birthday Girl

A baby's first birthday is a very special celebration and this cute card will mark the occasion perfectly.

Stitch count 33h x 32w
Design size 6 x 6cm (2⅜ x 2⅜in)

You will need
16 x 16cm (6¼ x 6¼in) 14-count white Aida ★
Size 26 tapestry needle ★
DMC threads as listed in chart key ★

For the stitching, use two strands for full and three-quarter cross stitch and one strand for French knots and for backstitch. See pages 98–99 if necessary.

To finish, trim the fabric edges with pinking shears and layer the stitching on to spotted paper. Place striped paper on to the front of a square single-fold card and stick the layered fabric on top with double-sided tape.

1st Birthday Boy

The silver outline stickers placed on to the embroidery gives added impact to this baby boy's first birthday card.

Stitch count 37h x 30w
Design size 6.7 x 5.4cm (2⅝in x 2⅛in)

You will need
★ 16 x 16cm (6¼ x 6¼in) 14-count white Aida
★ Size 26 tapestry needle
★ DMC threads as listed in chart key

For the stitching, use two strands for full and three-quarter cross stitch and one strand for French knots and for backstitch. See pages 98–99 if necessary.

To finish, trim the fabric edges with pinking shears. Stick patterned paper on to the front of a square single-fold card. Attach the fabric on top using double-sided tape. Add silver peel-off stars and a 'Birthday' sentiment to the embroidery.

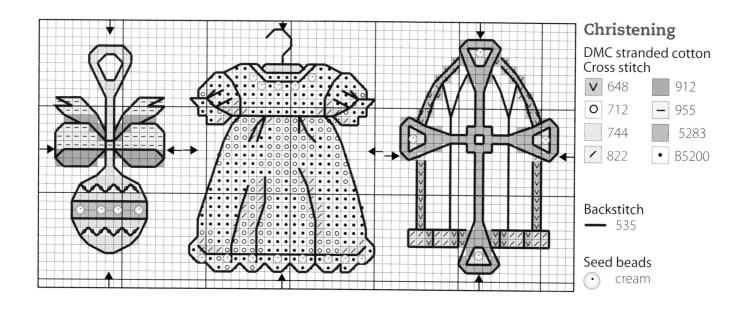

Christening

DMC stranded cotton
Cross stitch

V	648		912
O	712	—	955
	744		5283
/	822	•	B5200

Backstitch
— 535

Seed beads
⊙ cream

1st Birthday Boy

DMC stranded cotton
Cross stitch

O	353		702	V	745		948
	519		738		807	•	blanc
	666		743	/	828		

Backstitch   French knots
— 413   ● 413

1st Birthday Girl

DMC stranded cotton
Cross stitch

O	353	L	437		676	✕	741		3770
	413	/	602	\	712	V	963	•	blanc
	435		666		726		3708		

Backstitch   French knots
— 413   ● 413

Cards for Girls

The girls in your life will be delighted with the pretty designs in this chapter, with cards suitable for little sweethearts of all ages. Many of the cards are perfect for congratulations and good luck cards as well as birthdays; for example, the Ballet Star card could celebrate passing a dancing exam.

The cards can be personalized further by changing the ages and adding names using the charts on page 19. An 18th birthday card has been designed so that the numbers could also be changed to celebrate being a teenager (age 13) or the beginning of adolescence (age 16).

it's a girl thing

Make it special...

Soft sugary pinks and lilacs teamed with sparkling silver make the perfect girly embellishment. For older girls you could add sheer organza ribbons and a hint of glitter glue for a sophisticated touch. You should be able to find a wide range of embellishments on specific themes, such as dancing, music and shopping.

girly girl

Juggling Clown

This brightly coloured clown has been designed with younger children in mind. Personalize the card by changing the number using the chart provided opposite.

Stitch count 59h x 37w
Design size 10.7 x 6.7cm (4¼ x 2⅝in)

You will need

20.3 x 16.5cm (8 x 6½in) 14-count white Aida ★
Size 26 tapestry needle ★
DMC threads as listed in chart key ★

For the stitching, use two strands for full and three-quarter cross stitch and one strand for backstitch. See pages 98–99 if necessary. Backstitch the number of your choice.

To finish, back the fabric with iron-on interfacing, trim and layer on to pink card. Cover the front of a single-fold card with scrapbook papers (Sandylion) and glue on ric-rac braid to conceal the join between papers. Stick the layered fabric in place with double-sided tape.

Balloon Bear

A simple tag decorated with 3D stickers complements this sweet bear. If desired you could add an age number to the balloon using one of the backstitch charts in this chapter or stitch the child's name above the design using the chart provided opposite.

Stitch count 48h x 24w
Design size 8.7 x 4.4cm (3½ x 1¾in)

You will need

★ 17.8 x 14cm (7 x 5½in) 14-count white Aida
★ Size 26 tapestry needle
★ DMC threads as listed in chart key

For the stitching, use two strands for full and three-quarter cross stitch and one strand for backstitch. See pages 98–99 if necessary.

To finish, back the fabric with iron-on interfacing, trim and layer on to pink card. Cover the front of a single-fold base card with scrapbook paper (Rob & Bob Studios). Cut a tag shape from pink card and decorate with stickers (Sandylion) and organza ribbon. Use double-sided tape to stick the tag on to the right-hand side of the base card and the layered fabric on to the left.

Use this backstitch chart to change the number on the clown design

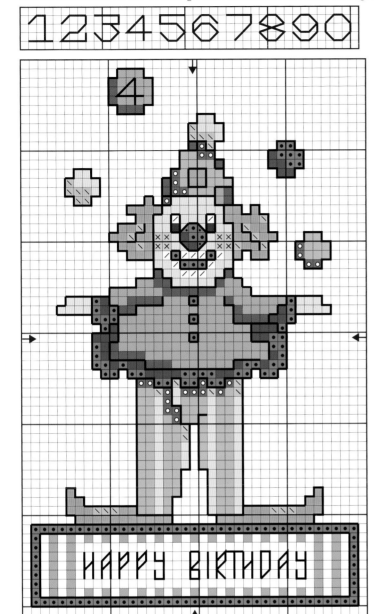

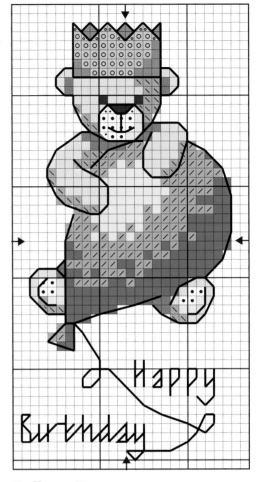

Balloon Bear

DMC stranded cotton
Cross stitch   **Backstitch**

■ 310	○ 604	□ 772
▨ 434	■ 700	• 819
⟍ 436	⟋ 703	▤ 963
■ 601	▨ 738	

Backstitch — 310

Juggling Clown

DMC stranded cotton
Cross stitch   **Backstitch**

■ 310	■ 699	⟍ 741	○ 995	⟋ B5200
■ 498	▨ 703	□ 743	▨ 996	
• 666	▨ 740	▤ 963	✕ 3716	

Backstitch — 310

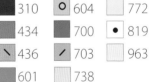

Use this backstitch chart to change the name and number on the Magical Unicorn design (pages 20–21). The alphabets could also be used to create your own messages for other designs in the book. Plan the letters on graph paper first to ensure they fit the space

Make a Wish

This pretty card could also be used as a congratulations card by using the chart on page 37 to stitch 'Congratulations' instead of 'Make a Wish'.

Stitch count 46h x 37w
Design size 8.3 x 6.7cm (3¼ x 2⅝in)

You will need

★ 17.8 x 16.5cm (7 x 6½in) 14-count white Aida
★ Size 26 tapestry needle
★ DMC threads as listed in chart key

For the stitching, use two strands for full and three-quarter cross stitch and one strand for backstitch. See pages 98–99 if necessary.

To finish, back the fabric with iron-on interfacing and trim. Cover the front of a single-fold card with scrapbook paper (Sandylion) and trim 1cm (⅜in) off the right-hand edge. Stick a 2cm (¾in) strip of lilac paper on the inside right-hand edge of the card. Attach the fabric to the front with double-sided tape and decorate with silver stars (Sandylion).

Fairy Fun

Stamps are perfect for adding a special touch to cards. You could make the card for a daughter, niece or any little girl by using the alphabet on page 19 to stitch the name.

Stitch count 57h x 33w
Design size 10.3 x 6cm (4 x 2⅜in)

You will need

17.8 x 15.2cm (7 x 6in) 14-count white Aida ★
Size 26 tapestry needle ★
DMC threads as listed in chart key ★

For the stitching, use two strands for full and three-quarter cross stitch and for French knots and use one strand for backstitch. See pages 98–99 if necessary.

To finish, back the fabric with iron-on interfacing, trim and layer on to pink card. Cover the front of a single-fold base card with scrapbook paper (Doodlebug). Stick the layered fabric on top and embellish with a tiara sticker (Habico).

Magical Unicorn

DMC Light Effects metallic threads and a coloured fabric give this card a magical touch. Glitter glue has been added to the fabric in places to enhance the sparkly effect.

Stitch count 42h x 28w
Design size 7.6 x 5.1cm (3 x 2in)

You will need

★ 15.2 x 12.7cm (6 x 5in) 14-count pale pink Aida (DMC 818)
★ Size 26 tapestry needle
★ DMC threads as listed in chart key

For the stitching, use two strands for full and three-quarter cross stitch and one strand for backstitch. See pages 98–99 if necessary. Backstitch the name and number of your choice using the chart on page 19.

To finish, back the fabric with iron-on interfacing, trim and layer on to pink card. Cover the front of a single-fold base card with scrapbook paper (Sandylion and Paper Adventures) and decorate with coordinating glitter stickers (Sandylion). Stick the layered fabric on top, embellish using glitter glue and allow to dry.

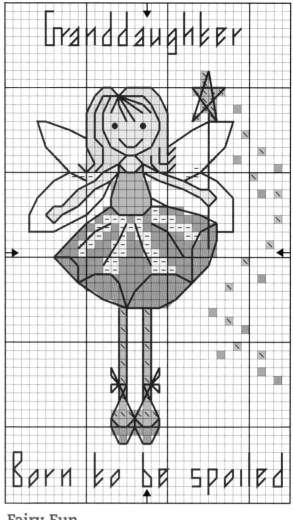

Make a Wish

DMC stranded cotton
Cross stitch   Backstitch

▨ 209	▨ 602	☐ 745	▨ E168	— 310
• 211	⁄ 742	＼ 963	(Light Effects)	

Fairy Fun

DMC stranded cotton
Cross stitch   Backstitch   French knots

▨ 208	▨ 744	— 3799	● 3799
− 211	▨ 963		
▨ 602	▨ 996		
＼ 740			

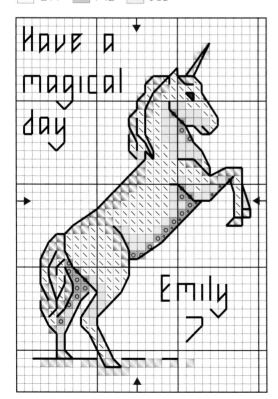

Magical Unicorn

DMC stranded cotton
Cross stitch   Backstitch

☐ 168	■ 310	▨ E168 (Light Effects)	— 310
⊙ 169	＼	▨ E3852 (Light Effects)	

See page 19 for the backstitch chart to change
the name and number on the design

Butterfly Greetings

This colourful card would suit any age and is great for all relatives, not just daughters – simply change the word using the chart on page 37. Pretty embellishments and gem stones add perfect finishing touches.

Stitch count 38h x 63w
Design size 6.9 x 11.4cm (2¾ x 4½in)

You will need

15.2 x 20.3cm (6 x 8in) 14-count white Aida ★
Size 26 tapestry needle ★
DMC threads as listed in chart key ★

For the stitching, use two strands for cross stitch and one strand for backstitch. See pages 98–99 if necessary.

To finish, back the fabric with iron-on interfacing and trim. Cover the bottom half of a single-fold card with scrapbook paper (Sandylion) and stick 3D flower stickers on to the top half. Cover the join with a strip of paper. Attach the fabric centrally to the base card using double-sided tape. Add adhesive gem stones (Papermania) to the butterfly wings and the flower centres.

Ballet Star

The birthday number on this lovely ballet-themed card can be changed using the chart provided opposite. If you omit the number the card would also be perfect to wish a young girl good luck in an exam.

Stitch count 50h x 32w
Design size 9 x 5.8cm (3½ x 2¼in)

You will need

★ 17.8 x 15.2cm (7 x 6in) 14-count white Aida
★ Size 26 tapestry needle
★ DMC threads as listed in chart key

For the stitching, use two strands for full and three-quarter cross stitch and one for backstitch. See pages 98–99 if necessary. Backstitch the number of your choice.

To finish, back the fabric with iron-on interfacing, trim and layer on to pink glitter card. Cover the front of a single-fold base card with ballet-themed paper (Sandylion). Stick the layered fabric on top using double-sided tape.

A Special Occasion

Iridescent Aida adds a special touch to this card. Numbers 3 and 6 are also charted so the card can celebrate a 13th or 16th birthday. See page 28 for a boy design.

Stitch count 40h x 32w (for design shown)
Design size 7.3 x 5.8cm (2⅞ x 2¼in)

You will need

17.8 x 15.2cm (7 x 6in) 14-count iridescent Aida (DMC DC27D) ★
Size 26 tapestry needle ★
DMC threads as listed in chart key ★

For the stitching, use two strands for full and three-quarter cross stitch and one strand for backstitch. See pages 98–99 if necessary.

To finish, back the fabric with iron-on interfacing, trim and layer on to pink and lilac card using double-sided tape. Cover the front of a single-fold base card with patterned papers (Dovecraft and Sandylion) and attach the layered fabric on to the card.

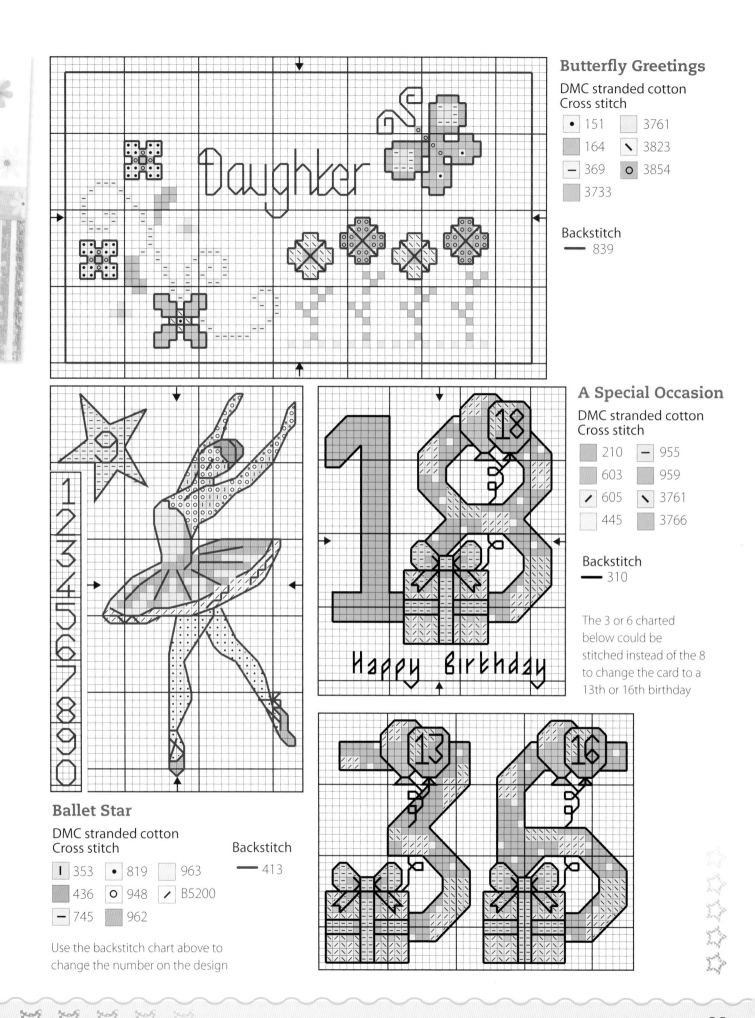

Butterfly Greetings

DMC stranded cotton
Cross stitch

•	151		3761
	164	\	3823
−	369	O	3854
	3733		

Backstitch
— 839

A Special Occasion

DMC stranded cotton
Cross stitch

	210	−	955
	603		959
/	605	\	3761
	445		3766

Backstitch
— 310

The 3 or 6 charted
below could be
stitched instead of the 8
to change the card to a
13th or 16th birthday

Ballet Star

DMC stranded cotton
Cross stitch

I	353	•	819		963
	436	O	948	/	B5200
−	745		962		

Backstitch
— 413

Use the backstitch chart above to
change the number on the design

Cards for Boys

In this chapter you will find a great range of terrific cards for boys of all ages – from a cheeky monkey to a biker boy. Some of the designs could also be used for sending congratulations or good luck as well as birthdays; for example, the Rock Star card could celebrate passing a music exam.

For birthday cards, you can change ages and add names using the charts provided and add other messages by using the alphabet charts on pages 37, 45 or 92. An 18th birthday card has been designed so that the number 8 could be replaced with a 6, to celebrate the beginning of adolescence at 16.

Make it special. . .

When choosing card decorations and embellishments for boys, look for bold, primary colours of blue, green, red and yellow to complement the cross stitch designs in this chapter. For older boys you could use 'shabby shades' and worn embellishments to give a more mature, grungy look. There are also plenty of themed embellishments to choose from – sports galore of course, plus music, adventure and animal themes.

Cheeky Monkey

This fun monkey has been designed with the younger child in mind. The birthday number is easily changed using the chart provided opposite.

Stitch count 36h x 21w
Design size 6.5 x 3.8cm (2½ x 1½in)

You will need

★ 15.2 x 12.7cm (6 x 5in) 14-count white Aida
★ Size 26 tapestry needle
★ DMC threads as listed in chart key

For the stitching, use two strands for full and three-quarter cross stitch and one strand for backstitch. See pages 98–99 if necessary. Backstitch the number of your choice.

To finish, back the fabric with iron-on interfacing, trim and layer on to blue and green card. Cover the front of a tall single-fold card with scrapbook paper (Sandylion and DCWV). Stick the layered fabric on to the base card. Attach a birthday-themed sticker on to striped card and then layer on to a strip of green card before sticking on to the front of the card.

Space Rocket

This design can be used for any young child's birthday simply by changing the number on the rocket using the chart provided opposite. You could use glow-in-the-dark stickers to add a fun element and the white thread could be replaced with DMC white glow-in-the-dark thread to enhance the surprise.

Stitch count 61h x 37w
Design size 11 x 6.7cm (4⅜ x 2⅝in)

You will need

20.3 x 15.2cm (8 x 6in) 14-count dark blue Aida ★
Size 26 tapestry needle ★
DMC threads as listed in chart key ★

For the stitching, use three strands for cross stitch, two strands for French knots and one strand for backstitch. See pages 98–99 if necessary. Backstitch the number of your choice.

To finish, back the fabric with iron-on interfacing, trim and layer on to yellow card. Decorate the front of a gate-fold card with space-themed paper (Craft House). Attach the layered fabric on the front left-hand panel, allowing the card to open.

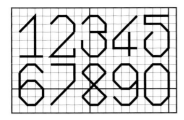

Use this backstitch chart to change the number on the design

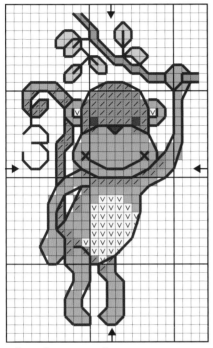

Cheeky Monkey

DMC stranded cotton
Cross stitch   **Backstitch**

■ 436	■ 905	— 838
V 543	■ 907	
■ 838	／ 3863	

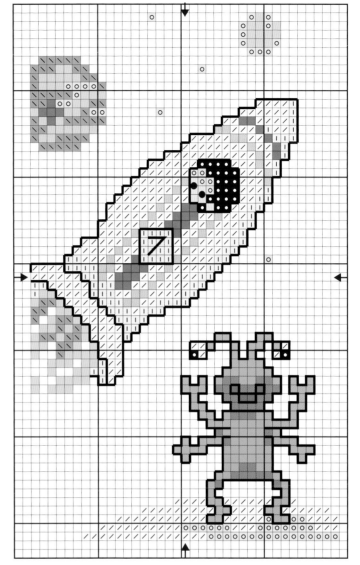

Space Rocket

DMC stranded cotton
Cross stitch   **Backstitch**

● 310	＼ 740	■ 963	— 310
■ 666	O 744	■ 3850	
■ 704	■ 809	／ B5200	**French knots**
■ 726	I 828		● 310

Use this backstitch chart
to change the number
on the rocket

Use this backstitch chart to change the
name and number on the Dragon Cake
design (page 28). The alphabets could also
be used to create your own messages for
other designs in the book. Plan the letters on
graph paper first to ensure they fit the space

Dragon Cake

This friendly dragon has been personalized with a name and age, which can be changed by using the chart on page 27.

Stitch count 51h x 38w
Design size 9.3 x 6.9cm (3⅝ x 2¾in)

You will need

17.8 x 15.2cm (7 x 6in) 14-count white Aida ★
Size 26 tapestry needle ★
DMC threads as listed in chart key ★

For the stitching, use two strands for full and three-quarter cross stitch and one strand for backstitch. See pages 98–99 if necessary. Backstitch the number of your choice.

To finish, back the fabric with iron-on interfacing, trim and layer on to pale blue card. Cover the front of a single-fold card with scrapbook paper (Sandylion). Glue printed ribbon (Doodlebug) across the bottom and then stick the layered fabric on to the front.

Football Mad

This bright design can be stitched for any sports-mad family member. Change the number using the chart opposite.

Stitch count 40h x 24w
Design size 7.3 x 4.4cm (2⅞ x 1¾in)

You will need

★ 17.8 x 12.7cm (7 x 5in) 14-count white Aida
★ Size 26 tapestry needle
★ DMC threads as listed in chart key

For the stitching, use two strands for full and three-quarter cross stitch and French knots and one strand for backstitch. See pages 98–99 if necessary. Backstitch the number of your choice.

To finish, back the fabric with iron-on interfacing and trim. Cover the front of a single-fold card with patterned paper (DCWV) and glue a rectangle of blue card on the front at an angle. Attach the fabric on top of the blue card using double-sided tape. Decorate with a football sticker to finish.

A Special Birthday

This special occasion card is stitched on fabric with an iridescent gleam, while DMC Memory thread creates streamers on the party popper. The number 6 is also provided so that the card could celebrate a 16th birthday. See page 22 for a girl design.

Stitch count 38h x 34w (for design shown)
Design size 6.9 x 6.2cm (2¾ x 2½in)

You will need

17.8 x 14cm (7 x 5½in) 14-count white iridescent Aida (DMC DC27D) ★
Size 26 tapestry needle ★
DMC threads as listed in chart key ★
DMC Desire memory thread 6150 ★

For the stitching, use two strands for full and three-quarter cross stitch and one strand for backstitch. See pages 98–99 if necessary. After pressing, stitch the Desire thread in place.

To finish, back the fabric with iron-on interfacing, trim and layer on to blue card. Cover the front of a single-fold card with scrapbook paper (Doodlebug). Stick the layered fabric on the left side of the card using double-sided tape. Layer a matching cake sticker on to orange and then blue card and attach using 3D foam pads.

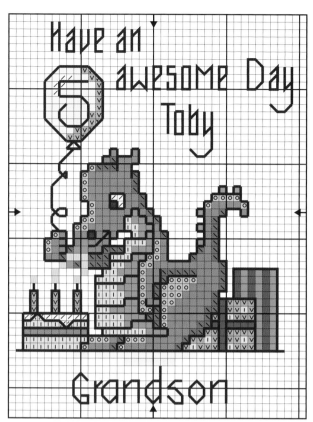

Use the backstitch chart to change the number

Dragon Cake

DMC stranded cotton
Cross stitch

		Backstitch
▨ 470	▨ 743	╲ 904	▮ 3855	— 838
⊙ 472	□ 747	⋁ 3766	╱ blanc	
▨ 517	▨ 838	▨ 3853		

See page 27 for the backstitch chart to change the name and number on the dragon design

Football Mad

DMC stranded cotton
Cross stitch

			Backstitch
▮ 666	▨ 726	✕ 3716	— 310
▨ 704	▨ 963	╱ B5200	**French knots**
			● 310

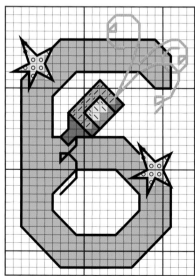

This 6 could be stitched instead of the 8 to change the card to a 16th birthday

A Special Birthday

DMC stranded cotton
Cross stitch

▨ 666
╱ 740
⊙ 745
▨ 911
╲ 955
▨ 996

Backstitch
— 310
— 995

DMC Desire memory thread
— 6150

Biker Boy

This is a useful card design suitable to many ages, which you could personalize by adding a name or age using the chart on page 27.

Stitch count 43h x 33w
Design size 7.8 x 6cm (3 x 2³/₈ in)

You will need

★ 17.8 x 15.2cm (7 x 6in) 14-count white Aida
★ Size 26 tapestry needle
★ DMC threads as listed in chart key

For the stitching, use two strands for full and three-quarter cross stitch and one strand for backstitch. See pages 98–99 if necessary.

To finish, back the fabric with iron-on interfacing, trim and layer on to red, then pale blue and then dark blue card. Attach the layered fabric on to a single-fold base card. Stick a strip of scrapbook paper (Making Memories) on the bottom half of the card and add a banner (Ali Craft).

Rock Star

This design would be ideal for an older boy (or girl). Add a name, age or message using the alphabet charts on pages 27 or 45.

Stitch count 29h x 22w
Design size 5.3 x 4cm (2 x 1½in)

You will need

15.2 x 14cm (6 x 5½in) 14-count white Aida ★
Size 26 tapestry needle ★
DMC threads as listed in chart key ★

For the stitching, use two strands for full and three-quarter cross stitch and one strand for backstitch. See pages 98–99 if necessary.

To finish, back the fabric with iron-on interfacing, trim and layer on to red card. Cover the front of a single-fold card with patterned paper (Dovecraft) and attach the layered fabric with double-sided tape. Musical embellishments (Craftime) add a finishing touch.

Cool Dude

The T-shirt in this design shows the child's age but this can be changed using the chart opposite. You could also change the colour of the T-shirt and skateboard.

Stitch count 42h x 34w
Design size 7.6 x 6.2cm (3 x 2½in)

You will need

★ 17.8 x 15.2cm (7 x 6in) 14-count white Aida
★ Size 26 tapestry needle
★ DMC threads as listed in chart key

For the stitching, use two strands for full and three-quarter cross stitch and French knots and one strand for backstitch. See pages 98–99 if necessary. Backstitch the number of your choice.

To finish, back the fabric with iron-on interfacing, trim and layer on to red card. Cover the front of a single-fold base card with denim-print paper (Sandylion). Create a simple pocket shape using the same paper. Add stitching lines in pen or use real stitching. Stick the denim pocket and the layered fabric in place using double-sided tape.

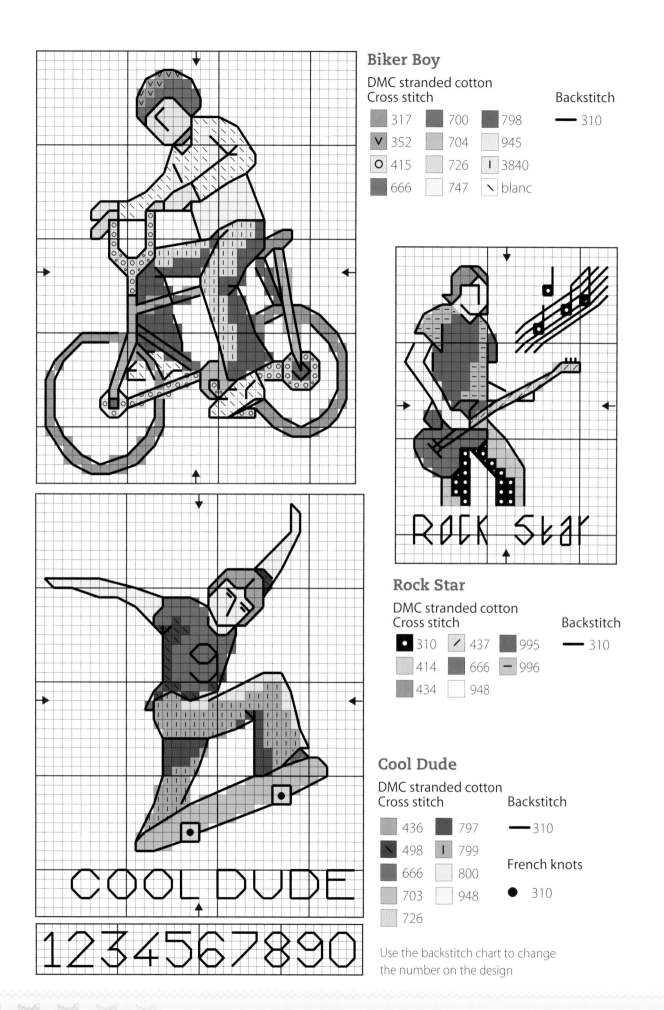

Biker Boy

DMC stranded cotton
Cross stitch

317	700	798
V 352	704	945
O 415	726	I 3840
666	747	\ blanc

Backstitch
— 310

Rock Star

DMC stranded cotton
Cross stitch

• 310	/ 437	995
414	666	– 996
434	948	

Backstitch
— 310

Cool Dude

DMC stranded cotton
Cross stitch

436	797
\ 498	I 799
666	800
703	948
726	

Backstitch
— 310

French knots
● 310

Use the backstitch chart to change
the number on the design

Cards for Women

This chapter focuses on the many women who hold valued places in our lives. There are some fabulous cards and they are very adaptable, so you will find something suitable for mum, grandma, aunt, sister, cousin, niece and friend.

There are also cards for important milestone birthdays and numbers and short messages have been charted to allow you to change the birthday number or personalize the designs further. For example, you could replace the words on the flower basket design overleaf with 'With Love', making the card suitable for any occasion. The Simply Fabulous card on page 36 could also be used for an 18th birthday by changing the wording.

Make it special...

Women today aren't easily pigeonholed so you are sure to find an array of embellishments that can be used to reflect each individual personality. You might choose delicate colours or go for a bright, bold scheme, depending on the recipient and the occasion. As well as the usual floral theme, why not experiment with fresh, contemporary embellishments?

Relax and Enjoy

For this fresh design, scrapbook papers and matching embellishments are used in soft colours. You could use the words charted on page 37 to add a different message.

Stitch count 33h x 47w
Design size 6 x 8.5cm (2³⁄₈ x 3³⁄₈in)

You will need

★ 15.2 x 19cm (6 x 7½in) 14-count white Aida
★ Size 26 tapestry needle
★ DMC threads as listed in chart key

For the stitching, use two strands for full and three-quarter cross stitch and one strand for backstitch. See pages 98–99 if necessary.

To finish, back the fabric with iron-on interfacing and trim. Layer the stitching on to pink scrapbook paper (Papermania). Cover a white single-fold card with pink and blue scrapbook paper and place a matching embellishment on the left-hand side. Stick the layered fabric on to the right-hand side.

Flower Basket

This pretty design could be stitched for other family members or friends by simply changing the text – see the chart on page 37 for some choices.

Stitch count 41h x 39w
Design size 7.5 x 7cm (3 x 2¾in)

You will need

17.8 x 17.8cm (7 x 7in) 14-count white Aida ★
Size 26 tapestry needle ★
DMC threads as listed in chart key ★

For the stitching, use two strands for full and three-quarter cross stitch and for French knots and one strand for backstitch. See pages 98–99 if necessary.

To finish, back the fabric with iron-on interfacing, trim and layer on to patterned paper. Use double-sided tape to stick this on a single-fold card covered with patterned paper (Papermania). Stick two cardstock squares (Papermania) on the left side of the card and stick embellishments (SandyLion) on the squares.

Present Time

A contemporary colour scheme of pink and brown forms the basis of this stylish card. Matching scrapbook papers are used to enhance the look.

Stitch count 42h x 42w
Design size 7.6 x 7.6cm (3 x 3in)

You will need

★ 17.8 x 17.8cm (7 x 7in) 14-count white Aida
★ Size 26 tapestry needle
★ DMC threads as listed in chart key

For the stitching, use two strands for full and three-quarter cross stitch and one strand for backstitch. See pages 98–99 if necessary.

To finish, back the fabric with iron-on interfacing, trim and then layer on to pink paper. Cover the front of a cream base card using patterned paper (Making Memories). Stick the layered fabric on to the card using double-sided tape.

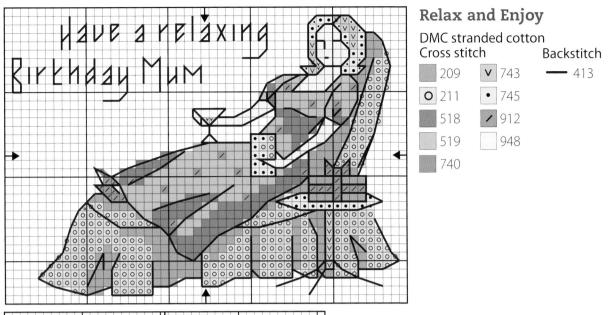

Have a relaxing
Birthday Mum

Relax and Enjoy

DMC stranded cotton

Cross stitch		Backstitch
▨ 209	V 743	— 413
O 211	• 745	
▨ 518	/ 912	
▨ 519	▨ 948	
▨ 740		

Happy Birthday Gran

Flower Basket

DMC stranded cotton

Cross stitch		Backstitch	French knots
/ 434	• 963	— 910	◔ 744
▨ 704	L 977	— 3031	
▨ 742	▨ 3746		
∧ 744	\ 3823		
— 910	▨ 3832		
▨ 957	▨ 3840		

Present Time

DMC stranded cotton

Cross stitch		Backstitch
× 151	▨ 948	— 3371
\ 543	V 3350	— 3862
▨ 899	▨ 3862	
▨ 938		

For a special

Sister

Tres Chic

This card uses pretty lilacs and bold patterns for impact. A tag made from matching scrapbook paper unifies the design. The chart opposite can be used to change the number or add other messages as desired.

Stitch count 56h x 31w
Design size 10.2 x 5.6cm (4 x 2¼in)

You will need

17.8 x 12.7cm (7 x 5in) 14-count white Aida ★
Size 26 tapestry needle ★
DMC threads as listed in chart key ★

For the stitching, use two strands for full and three-quarter cross stitch and one strand for backstitch. See pages 98–99 if necessary.

To finish, back the fabric with iron-on interfacing, trim and add a crystal brad (Making Memories) to the stitched bag. Layer the fabric on to lilac paper using double-sided tape. Cover the left-hand side of a white single-fold card with scrapbook paper and ribbon and stick the fabric on top. Cut the same paper into a tag shape and decorate with ribbon and paper blossoms (Making Memories). Stick a metal charm (Making Memories) on the paper blossom.

Simply Fabulous

Striking patterned papers are used to complement this sassy card. For a different look, change the papers to softer or even metallic tones – fabulous, whatever the age of the recipient. Use the chart opposite to change the number or add messages.

Stitch count 40h x 31w
Design size 7.3 x 5.6cm (2⅞ x 2¼in)

You will need

★ 17.8 x 12.7cm (7 x 5in) 14-count white Aida
★ Size 26 tapestry needle
★ DMC threads as listed in chart key

For the stitching, use two strands for full and three-quarter cross stitch and for French knots and one strand for backstitch. See pages 98–99 if necessary.

To finish, back the fabric with iron-on interfacing, trim and then layer on to patterned paper. Cover the front of a white single-fold card with scrapbook paper (Provo Craft) and use black ribbon to conceal the join. Stick the layered fabric on the front of the card. Place adhesive gem stones (Papermania) on to the bottom corners of the fabric and a matching 3D sticker (Provo Craft) at the bottom right-hand side of the card.

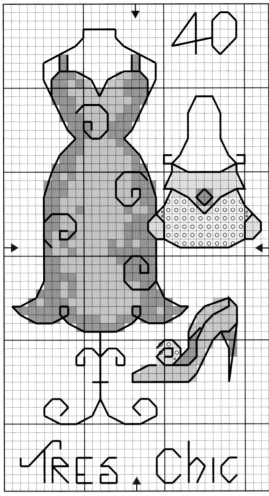

Simply Fabulous

DMC stranded cotton
Cross stitch

Cross stitch			Backstitch	French knots
437	666	948	— 310	● 310
O 498	– 677			

Tres Chic

DMC stranded cotton
Cross stitch   Backstitch

Cross stitch	Backstitch
210	— 310
553	
726	
O 3078	

0123456789 With Love
For my Mum Daughter
Mother Auntie
Niece Cousin
Step Sister
Grandma Nan
Best Friend Wishes
Congratulations
Well Done Get Well

You can use this backstitch chart to change the words or create your own messages on the cards in this section, or for any of the cards in the book

Mother's Day

A box of chocolates and a domed Mum sticker makes this card perfect for Mother's Day, but it could be also sent to other female family members by using the chart on page 37 to change the wording to, for example, 'For My Grandma'.

Stitch count 37h x 38w
Design size 6.8 x 6.8cm (2¾ x 2¾in)

You will need

★ 15.2 x 15.2cm (6 x 6in) 14-count iridescent Aida (DMC DC27D)
★ Size 26 tapestry needle
★ DMC threads as listed in chart key

For the stitching, use two strands for full and three-quarter cross stitch and one strand for backstitch. See pages 98–99 if necessary.

To finish, back the fabric with iron-on interfacing and then trim and layer on to patterned paper. Stick this on to a pink single-fold card using double-sided tape, then place a ribbon and a dome sticker (Papermania) towards the bottom of the card.

Vase of Flowers

This fresh, contemporary design has adhesive gem stones added to the centre of the flowers to create a 3D quality to the card. You could change the word 'friend' using the chart on page 37.

Stitch count 52h x 35w
Design size 9.4 x 6.4cm (3¾ x 2½in)

You will need

17.8 x 14cm (7 x 5½in) 14-count white Aida ★
Size 26 tapestry needle ★
DMC threads as listed in chart key ★

For the stitching, use two strands for cross stitch and one strand for backstitch. See pages 98–99 if necessary.

To finish, back the fabric with iron-on interfacing, trim and layer on to a pale blue base card. Place adhesive gems (Papermania) on to the centre of the flowers. Stick white ric-rac on to the vase and add a blue adhesive gem stone.

Vintage Style

This nostalgic card would be suitable for many occasions. 3D stickers echo the stitched flowers. You could use the chart on page 37 to add a personal message.

Stitch count 32h x 49w
Design size 5.8 x 8.9cm (2¼ x 3½in)

You will need

★ 15.2 x 17.8cm (6 x 7in) 14-count white Aida
★ Size 26 tapestry needle
★ DMC threads as listed in chart key

For the stitching, use two strands for full and three-quarter cross stitch and for French knots and one strand for backstitch. See pages 98–99 if necessary.

To finish, back the fabric with iron-on interfacing, trim and then layer on to patterned paper (Anna Griffin). Cover the front of a single-fold card with coordinating paper. Stick the layered fabric on the card using double-sided tape and embellish with a dome sticker and 3D flower sticker (K&Co).

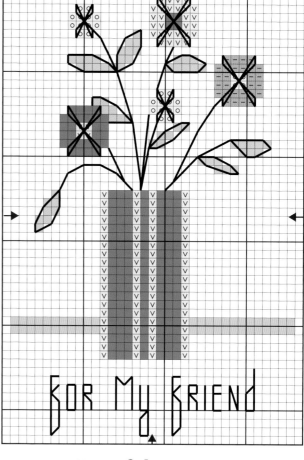

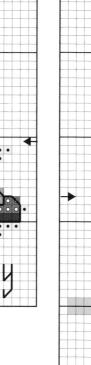

Mother's Day

DMC stranded cotton
Cross stitch

			Backstitch
− 605	938	3838	— 3371
743	943	O 3840	
• 745	961	/ blanc	
⊙ 840	964		

Vase of Flowers

DMC stranded cotton
Cross stitch

			Backstitch
743	798	V 800	— 310
O 745	− 799	913	

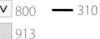

Vintage Style

DMC stranded cotton
Cross stitch

/ 211	519	⊡ 838
310	553	948
347	702	− 962
434	743	O 963
\ 437	∧ 745	

Backstitch   French knots

— 310   ⦿ 743

═ B5200   O B5200

Cards for Men

This chapter has some great cards for the many wonderful men in our lives. The designs are versatile, allowing them to be used for many recipients and occasions; for example, the World's Best Dad card could also be used for Father's Day by omitting the Happy Birthday words. Themes include sports, racing cars, gardening, football and party time.

Milestone 40th and 50th birthdays are celebrated with eye-catching designs and all of the cards can be personalized by adding names, dates and ages using the charts provided. You could also use the charts on pages 37, 45 and 92 to create and stitch your own messages.

Make it special...

Today, choosing colour schemes and card embellishments for the men in your life couldn't be easier. Sports and gardening embellishments are easy to find as well as masculine-themed stickers. Choose bold, bright colours and striking prints for eye-catching cards, picking out the colours from the charted designs and using these in the embellishments to unify the finished card.

World's Best Dad

Bold football-themed motifs decorate the letters DAD to make a simple yet striking card. The design could be changed to suit Father's Day by omitting the words 'Happy Birthday'.

Stitch count 37h x 68w
Design size 6.7 x 12.3cm (2⅝ x 4⅞in)

You will need

17.8 x 23cm (7 x 9in) 14-count white Aida ★
Size 26 tapestry needle ★
DMC threads as listed in chart key ★

For the stitching, use two strands for full and three-quarter cross stitch and one strand for backstitch. See pages 98–99 if necessary.

To finish, back the fabric with iron-on interfacing, trim and layer on to red card. Cover the bottom half of a single-fold base card with scrapbook paper (English Paper Company) and stick the layered fabric on top.

Grandad's Shed

The humorous theme of this card is echoed by the fun hosepipe sticker, although this can be replaced with another garden-themed embellishment if desired.

Stitch count 53h x 47w
Design size 9.6 x 8.5cm (3¾ x 3⅜in)

You will need

★ 20.3 x 17.8cm (8 x 7in) 14-count Aida
★ Size 26 tapestry needle
★ DMC threads as listed in chart key

For the stitching, use two strands for full and three-quarter cross stitch and for French knots and one strand for backstitch. See pages 98–99 if necessary.

To finish, back the fabric with iron-on interfacing, trim and layer on to green card. Cover the front of a single-fold card with patterned paper (DCWV) and a strip of orange card. Attach the layered fabric on top using double-sided tape. Stick the hosepipe embellishment (Craft for Occasions) on to the bottom of the card.

Number 1 Brother

A bold colour scheme was used for this card. Make the design suitable for another family member by using the chart on page 45 to change the word.

Stitch count 51h x 25w
Design size 9.3 x 4.5cm (3⅝ x 1¾in)

You will need

17.8 x 12.7cm (7 x 5in) 14-count Aida ★
Size 26 tapestry needle ★
DMC threads as listed in chart key ★

For the stitching, use two strands for full and three-quarter cross stitch and one strand for backstitch. See pages 98–99 if necessary.

To finish, trim the fabric and cover the front of an oval aperture double-fold card with red and grey papers (DCWV). Mount the fabric in the card using double-sided tape.

World's Best Dad

DMC stranded cotton
Cross stitch

⊡	310
○	415
	436
	666
⟍	676
∨	677
	798
⁄	B5200

Backstitch

—— 310

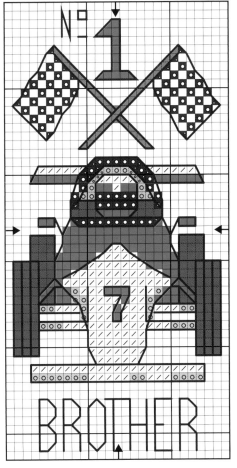

Grandad's Shed

DMC stranded cotton
Cross stitch

○	168		604	•	712	∨	741		840
⁄	435		701		726	I	747		3825
	519		704	L	738	⟍	772		

Backstitch

—— 310

French knots

● 310

Number 1 Brother

DMC stranded cotton
Cross stitch

⊡	310		436
○	318		666
	413	⁄	B5200

Backstitch

—— 310

Put on Your Party Pants!

This card has been finished as a 40th birthday card but the message is the same whatever the age, so have some fun! The glitter numbers are easily changed to suit different ages.

Stitch count 32h x 62w
Design size 5.8 x 11.2cm (2¼ x 4⅜in)

You will need

★ 15.2 x 20.3cm (6 x 8in) 14-count white Aida
★ Size 26 tapestry needle
★ DMC threads as listed in chart key
★ DMC Desire memory thread 6070

For the stitching, use two strands for full and three-quarter cross stitch and for the French knot and one strand for backstitch. See pages 98–99 if necessary. After pressing, stitch the Desire thread into place.

To finish, back the fabric with iron-on interfacing, trim and layer on to patterned paper. Cover a single-fold base card with scrapbook paper (Provo Craft). Layer a rectangle of white card on to red card and embellish with glitter numbers (Express Yourself D.I.Y). Attach Desire thread and a clothes peg to the top of the number 4. Stick the layered fabric and numbers to the front of the card using double-sided tape.

Fizzing at 50

DMC Light Effects thread adds a metallic gold sparkle to this contemporary-styled card.

Stitch count 35h x 40w
Design size 6.4 x 7.3cm (2½ x 2⅞in)

You will need

14 x 15.2cm (5½ x 6in) 14-count white Aida ★
Size 26 tapestry needle ★
DMC threads as listed in chart key ★

For the stitching, use two strands for full and three-quarter cross stitch and one for backstitch. See pages 98–99 if necessary.

To finish, back the fabric with iron-on interfacing, trim and layer on to pale blue card using double-sided tape. Cover the bottom half of the front of a yellow single-fold card with striped paper (Sandylion). Decorate by attaching green ribbon to the top edge. Fix the layered fabric centrally to the front of the card.

Put on Your Party Pants!

DMC stranded cotton
Cross stitch

▨ 519	I 702	T 742	▨ 3838
▪ 666	▨ 704	O 747	▨ 3840
▪ 699	▨ 738	▪ 797	⁄ B5200

Backstitch
— 310
— 797

French knot
● 310

DMC Desire memory thread
▬ 6070

Use this backstitch chart to change the words and numbers on your cards, or to create your own messages

Fizzing at 50

DMC stranded cotton
Cross stitch

● 310	▪ 700	▨ 740	▪ 995	⁄ B5200
V 435	▨ 703	▨ 743	▨ 996	▨ E3821 (Light Effects)

Backstitch
— 310

It's a Hard Life

Green and blue papers echo the colours in the design creating further harmony. The design is a versatile one – change the wording using the alphabets and words charted on pages 37 and 45.

Stitch count 31h x 46w
Design size 5.6 x 8.3cm (2¼ x 3¼in)

You will need

★ 15.2 x 17.8cm (6 x 7in) 14-count white Aida
★ Size 26 tapestry needle
★ DMC threads as listed in chart key

For the stitching, use two strands for full and three-quarter cross stitch and one strand for backstitch. See pages 98–99 if necessary.

To finish, back the fabric with iron-on interfacing, trim and layer on to blue card. Glue a rectangle of green card to the front of a patterned, square single-fold card (DCWV). Attach the layered fabric to the card and stick the 'DAD' and flag embellishments (Sandylion) on to the bottom-right corner.

Birthday Celebration

Desire memory thread was used to create the balloon string but craft wire could also have been used. The card could be stitched for any family member using the chart on page 45.

Stitch count 38h x 46w
Design size 6.9 x 8.3cm (2¾ x 3¼in)

You will need

17.8 x 17.8cm (7 x 7in) 14-count white Aida ★
Size 26 tapestry needle ★
DMC threads as listed in chart key ★
DMC Desire memory thread 6100 ★

For the stitching, use two strands for full and three-quarter cross stitch and one strand for backstitch. See pages 98–99 if necessary. Couch the Desire thread in place after pressing the fabric.

To finish, back the fabric with iron-on interfacing, trim and layer on to yellow card. Stick patterned papers (DCWV) on to the front of a square single-fold blue base card. Attach the layered fabric on top. Add two silver star embellishments (Sandylion) for the finishing touch.

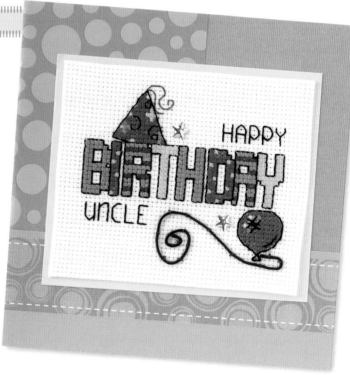

Time for Cricket

The card has been personalized for a nephew by adding alphabet stickers. A miniature cricket bat, stumps and ball provide a 3D element.

Stitch count 34h x 29w
Design size 6.2 x 5.2cm (2½ x 2in)

You will need

★ 16.5 x 12.7cm (6½ x 5in) pale green 14-count Aida (DMC 772)
★ Size 26 tapestry needle
★ DMC threads as listed in chart key

For the stitching, use three strands for full and three-quarter cross stitch and one strand for backstitch. See pages 98–99 if necessary.

To finish, trim the fabric and mount within a square aperture double-fold yellow card using double-sided tape. Stick a strip of blue paper to the bottom of the card. Layer a narrower strip of white paper on to the blue and then add the letters (DCWV) and cricket bat embellishment (Paper Cellar).

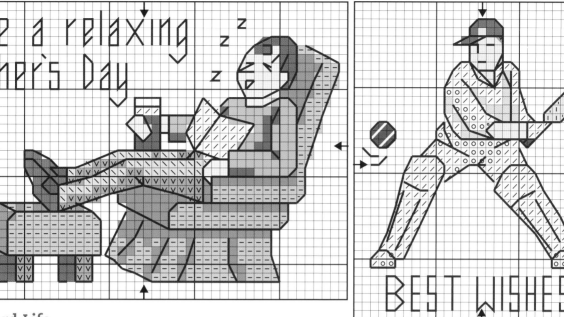

It's a Hard Life

DMC stranded cotton
Cross stitch

				Backstitch
− 164	v 436	995	/ B5200	— 310
320	\ 738	996		
433	948	3350		

Time for Cricket

DMC stranded cotton
Cross stitch

			Backstitch
321	726	995	— 310
415	I 738	/ B5200	⚊ B5200
v 435	951	o ecru	

Birthday Celebration

DMC stranded cotton
Cross stitch

- 700
- o 704
- 726
- 798
- • 996

Backstitch

— 310

— 700

DMC Desire memory thread

— 6100

People with Passions

Most of us are passionate about something and knowing what sets someone's heart racing or soothes them after a long day means that you can create just the right card for them. This chapter covers some popular passions, including music, gardening, DIY, cooking, pets and even shopping.

Your hand-stitched greetings can be made even more special and personal by adding names and messages to the designs using the backstitch charts on pages 37, 45 and 92, and you will have a lot of fun enhancing the cards by choosing fun embellishments that reflect the passion.

Make it special. . .

There are embellishments to fit almost any occasion and people with passions are no exception. You will find decorative elements that will appeal to people passionate about gardening, music, embroidery, sports, pets, cooking, DIY, shopping and much more. Choose embellishments to suit their passion and select colours to match or contrast with the shades used in the cross stitch.

For a DIY Enthusiast

This is a great card for DIY enthusiasts. You could personalize the card by changing the wording to the name of the recipient or add a message of your own using the alphabets charted on pages 37, 45 or 92.

Stitch count 42h x 18w
Design size 7.6 x 3.3cm (3 x 1¼in)

You will need
15.2 x 12.7cm (6 x 5in) 14-count white Aida ★
Size 26 tapestry needle ★
DMC threads as listed in chart key ★

For the stitching, use two strands for full and three-quarter cross stitch and French knots and one strand for backstitch. See pages 98–99 if necessary.

To finish, back the fabric with iron-on interfacing, trim and layer on to orange card. Add a strip of patterned paper (Making Memories) to the bottom of a single-fold blue base card. Stick an orange strip across the top to conceal the join. Stick the layered fabric on the card and a metal charm (Making Memories) on the orange strip.

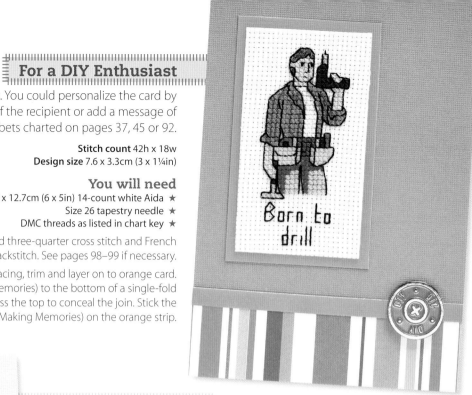

For a Special Teacher

This heart-warming sentiment would be perfect for a special teacher. The quote by E. E. Cummings on the card front would also make a wonderful sentiment if backstitched using the alphabet on page 27.

Stitch count 43h x 33w
Design size 7.6 x 6cm (3 x 2⅜in)

You will need
★ 15.2 x 15.2cm (6 x 6in) 14-count white Aida
★ Size 26 tapestry needle
★ DMC threads as listed in chart key

For the stitching, use two strands for full and three-quarter cross stitch and French knots. Use two strands for white backstitch and one strand for black. See pages 98–99 if necessary.

To finish, back the fabric with iron-on interfacing, trim and layer on to pink card. Stick a strip of patterned paper (Sandylion) across the bottom of a single-fold pink base card. Attach the layered fabric on to the base card using double-sided tape.

For a Music Lover

This stylish card would suit anyone who loves music and could also be used to send congratulations for passing a music exam.

Stitch count 32h x 35w
Design size 5.8 x 6.3cm (2¼ x 2½in)

You will need
15.2 x 15.2cm (6 x 6in) 14-count white Aida ★
Size 26 tapestry needle ★
DMC threads as listed in chart key ★

For the stitching, use two strands for full and three-quarter cross stitch and one strand for backstitch. See pages 98–99 if necessary.

To finish, back the fabric with iron-on interfacing, trim and layer on to gold card. Stick scrapbook paper (Sandylion) on the front of a single-fold base card. Attach the layered fabric on top and then glue a music embellishment (Craftime) on to the card for decoration.

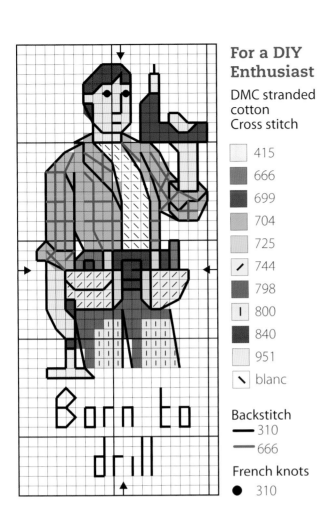

For a DIY Enthusiast

DMC stranded cotton
Cross stitch

☐	415
▨	666
▨	699
☐	704
☐	725
⁄	744
▨	798
I	800
▨	840
☐	951
＼	blanc

Backstitch
— 310
— 666

French knots
● 310

For a Special Teacher

DMC stranded cotton
Cross stitch

								Backstitch
☐	164	▨	602	☐	948			— 310
⊙	310	○	605	▨	987			(1 strand)
•	352	＼	738	▨	3839			— blanc
☐	436	V	800					(2 strands)

French knots
● 310

For a Music Lover

DMC stranded cotton
Cross stitch

				Backstitch
⊙	310	•	436	— 310
▨	317	○	840	
＼	415		948	
▨	434	⁄	B5200	

For a Shopaholic

Shopping has to be one of our favourite pastimes so this card is sure to suit someone you know.

Stitch count 46h x 29w
Design size 8.3 x 5.2cm (3¼ x 2in)

You will need

★ 17.8 x 12.7cm (7 x 5in) 14-count white Aida
★ Size 26 tapestry needle
★ DMC threads as listed in chart key

For the stitching, use two strands for full and three-quarter cross stitch and French knots and one strand for backstitch. See pages 98–99 if necessary.

To finish, back the fabric with iron-on interfacing, trim and layer on to patterned paper. Cover the front of a single-fold base card with coordinating paper (Doodlebug) and then stick the layered fabric centrally on to the front of the card.

For Gardeners

Fun seed-packet embellishments and brads add attractive finishing touches to this gardening-themed card.

Stitch count 50h x 33w
Design size 9 x 6cm (3½ x 2⅜in)

You will need

17.8 x 14cm (7 x 5½in) 14-count white Aida ★
Size 26 tapestry needle ★
DMC threads as listed in chart key ★

For the stitching, use two strands for full and three-quarter cross stitch and French knots and one strand for backstitch. See pages 98–99 if necessary.

To finish, back the fabric with iron-on interfacing, trim and secure brads through the top corners. Cover the front of a single-fold base card with scrapbook paper (Sandylion) and stick the fabric centrally on top. Decorate by attaching seed packet embellishments (Craft for Occasions) on the bottom right-hand corner of the fabric.

For the Best Cook

This is the ideal card for those who love to cook. A chef's hat and utensils are a fun finishing touch.

Stitch count 30h x 19w
Design size 5.4 x 3.4cm (2⅛ x 1⅜in)

You will need

★ 15.2 x 12.7cm (6 x 5in) 14-count white Aida
★ Size 26 tapestry needle
★ DMC threads as listed in chart key

For the stitching, use two strands for full and three-quarter cross stitch and French knots and one strand for backstitch. See pages 98–99 if necessary.

To finish, back the fabric with iron-on interfacing, trim and layer on to dark blue card. Attach cooking-themed embellishments (Craft for Occasions) on to the left-hand side of the blue card. Cover the front of a single-fold base card with gingham print paper and stick the dark blue card on top.

For a Shopaholic

DMC stranded cotton
Cross stitch

			Backstitch	French knots
602	743	/ 970	— 310	● 310
700	948	O 3716		
704	964	O 3812		

For Gardeners

DMC stranded cotton
Cross stitch

			Backstitch
164	O 722	O 987	— 310
V 168	T 741	I 3825	
436	744	3839	French knots
603	948	/ 3840	● 310
700	— 964	\ blanc	

For the Best Cook

DMC stranded cotton
Cross stitch

		Backstitch	French knots
310	797	— 310	● 310
349	948		
437	/ B5200		
O 676			

For Cat Lovers

For cat lovers, these cat-themed embellishments on this cute card are just purr-fect!

Stitch count 41h x 33w
Design size 7.5 x 6cm (3 x 2⅜in)

You will need

15.2 x 14cm (6 x 5½in) 14-count white Aida ★
Size 26 tapestry needle ★
DMC threads as listed in chart key ★

For the stitching, use two strands for full and three-quarter cross stitch and one strand for backstitch. See pages 98–99 if necessary.

To finish, trim the fabric, layer on to scrapbook paper (Provo Craft) and stick on to the left-hand side of a pink single-fold card. Cover the right-hand side with the same paper. Cut two squares from pink card and stick on to the patterned paper. Add embellishments (Sandylion) to the squares and on to the left-hand side of the card below the stitching.

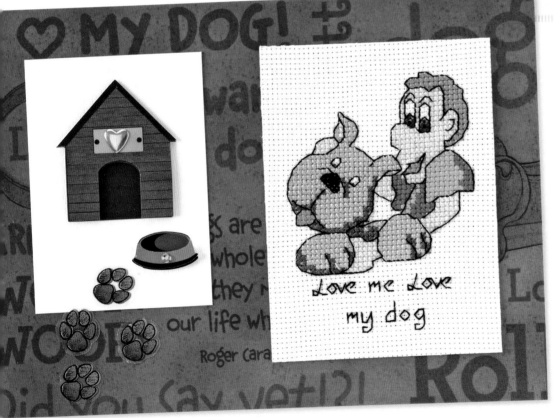

For Dog Lovers

'Love me, love my dog' is a great sentiment for this bold card. A kennel, dog bowl and paw prints provide fun finishing touches.

Stitch count 51h x 39w
Design size 9.3 x 7cm (3⅝ x 2¾in)

You will need

★ 17.8 x 15.2cm (7 x 6in) 14-count white Aida
★ Size 26 tapestry needle
★ DMC threads as listed in chart key

For the stitching, use two strands for full and three-quarter cross stitch and French knots and one strand for backstitch. See pages 98–99 if necessary.

To finish, back the fabric with iron-on interfacing and trim. Cover a single-fold card with scrapbook paper (Sandylion). Stick the fabric on to the right-hand side of the card and glue a rectangle of white card on to the left-hand side. Decorate the white card using dog-themed stickers (Sandylion and Paper Cellar).

For Cat Lovers

DMC stranded cotton
Cross stitch

↘	211
	335
	340
	519
•	819
	963
⁄	blanc

Backstitch

—— 317

For Dog Lovers

DMC stranded cotton
Cross stitch

⊡	310
	351
⊙	352
	436
	817
	839
	948
v	3790
	3864
↘	blanc

Backstitch

—— 310

French knots

● 310

Love and Romance

Love and romance are at the heart of so many occasions in our lives and Valentine's Day, engagements, weddings and wedding anniversaries are celebrated in this chapter. You will find both traditional and contemporary designs – from a bride and groom and red roses to a mischievous cupid and sentimental teddy.

Some of the anniversary cards can be personalized using the alphabet and numerals provided, while the colour schemes of the wedding cards can be changed to match the theme of the wedding. A pair of pretty love birds can be used for any romantic occasion.

Make it special. . .
Love certainly makes the world go round and you will find masses of embellishments available to decorate your romantic cards, including hearts, flowers, wedding rings, Champagne glasses and doves. Choose soft, romantic colours such as cream, aqua and lilac, or go bold with zesty reds and bright pinks. Adding tiny accents of metallic gold or silver can work well too and gives cards an extra sparkle.

Missing you

Congratulations on your Engagement

Valentine be mine

10
Wedding Anniversary

Wedding Day

Forever

Engagement

Fresh, contemporary colours and bold motifs are combined to produce this stylish engagement card.

Stitch count 60h x 34w
Design size 10.9 x 6.2cm (4¼ x 2½in)

You will need

★ 20.3 x 15.2cm (8 x 6in) 14-count white Aida
★ Size 26 tapestry needle
★ DMC threads as listed in chart key

For the stitching, use two strands for full and three-quarter cross stitch and one strand for backstitch. See pages 98–99 if necessary.

To finish, trim the fabric and mount within a rectangular aperture double-fold card. Glue a 5cm (2in) strip of patterned paper to the bottom of the front of the card and trim around the aperture. Attach a metal heart (Papermania) to the bottom corner of the fabric using a silver brad.

Contemporary Wedding

A soft lilac and cream colour scheme is the basis for this modern wedding card, with the wedding rings stitched in gold Light Effects thread for extra sparkle.

Stitch count 32h x 39w
Design size 5.8 x 7cm (2¼ x 2¾in)

You will need

15.2 x 17.8cm (6 x 7in) 14-count pale cream Aida ★
Size 26 tapestry needle ★
DMC threads as listed in chart key ★

For the stitching, use two strands for cross stitch and one strand for backstitch. See pages 98–99 if necessary.

To finish, trim the fabric with pinking shears. Cover a single-fold card with patterned paper and stick the fabric patch on top using double-sided tape. Stick an oval-shaped embellishment (Crafty Bitz) on the left side as a finishing touch.

Traditional Wedding

This delightful traditional image of a bride and groom was stitched on iridescent Aida for a special look.

Stitch count 64h x 35w
Design size 11.6 x 6.3cm (4½ x 2½in)

You will need

★ 20.3 x 15.2cm (8 x 6in) 14-count white iridescent Aida (DMC DC27D)
★ Size 26 tapestry needle
★ DMC threads as listed in chart key

For the stitching, use two strands for full and three-quarter cross stitch and for French knots. Use one strand for backstitch. See pages 98–99 if necessary.

To finish, trim the fabric with pinking shears and layer on to blue card. Wrap ribbon around cream embossed card and stick to the front of a single-fold blue base card. Stick the fabric on top using double-sided tape. Place a tag and paper rose (Crafty Bitz) at the bottom.

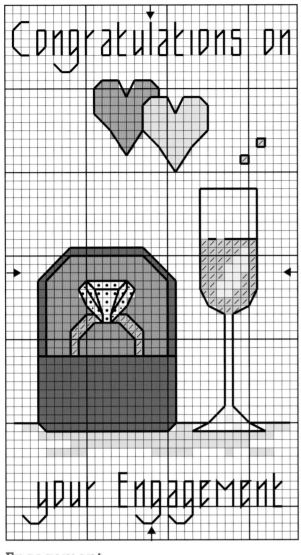

Engagement

DMC stranded cotton
Cross stitch

▨ 602	╱ 676	▨ 797	Backstitch
▨ 605	▨ 745	• B5200	── 3799

Traditional Wedding

DMC stranded cotton
Cross stitch

▨ 164	▨ 434	v 745	▨ 3731
╲ 168	O 676	▢ 948	▨ 3799
▨ 318	▨ 677	╱ 962	• B5200
▬ 414	▨ 702	× 963	

Backstitch
── 3799

French knots
● 3731
● 3799

Contemporary Wedding

DMC stranded cotton
Cross stitch

▨ 210	▨ 745	▨ E3852	Backstitch
▨ 553	╲ 746	(Light Effects)	── 3799

Anniversary Rose

Various shades of pink and the embellishments used in this design create a very pretty card. The number can be changed to suit the relevant anniversary. You could also add initials using the chart opposite to personalize the card further.

Stitch count 69h x 40w
Design size 12.5 x 7.3cm (5 x 2⁷⁄₈in)

You will need
★ 23 x 17.8cm (9 x 7in) 14-count white Aida
★ Size 26 tapestry needle
★ DMC threads as listed in chart key

For the stitching, use two strands for cross stitch and one strand for backstitch. See pages 98–99 if necessary. Use the chart provided to change the number on the card.

To finish, back the fabric with iron-on interfacing and trim before layering on to patterned paper. Stick two rectangles of coloured card on to the front of a single-fold base card. Stick the layered fabric on top using double-sided tape. Place a 1cm (³⁄₈in) wide strip of coloured card at the bottom of the card and stick a 'Forever' sticker (Dovecraft) and wine glasses (K&Co) on top.

Anniversary Sampler

Rows of repeated motifs are used in this traditional band sampler, enhanced by imaginative embellishments.

Stitch count 58h x 35w
Design size 10.5 x 6.4cm (4¹⁄₈ x 2½in)

You will need
20.3 x 15.2cm (8 x 6in) 14-count white Aida ★
Size 26 tapestry needle ★
DMC threads as listed in chart key ★

For the stitching, use two strands for cross stitch and one strand for backstitch. See pages 98–99 if necessary. Use the chart opposite to personalize the design.

To finish, back the fabric with iron-on interfacing and trim. Cover a single-fold card with a strip of patterned paper and ribbon. Stick the fabric patch on to matching paper before sticking on to the card with double-sided tape. Secure a paper flower (Prima) with a gold brad and fix on the right side, placing a tag (Crafty Bitz) next to the flower.

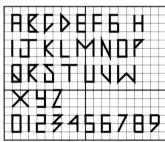

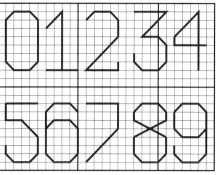

Use these backstitch numerals to change the number on the Anniversary Rose card

Anniversary Rose

DMC stranded cotton

Cross stitch		Backstitch
■ 350	− 818	— 844
╱ 352	▨ 910	
○ 353	▨ 913	
▢ 745	▨ 3716	

Use this alphabet and numerals chart to personalize the Anniversary Sampler

Anniversary Sampler

DMC stranded cotton
Cross stitch

▨ 155	╲ 676	╱ 3716
+ 168	▢ 745	
▨ 602	○ 818	

Backstitch
— 3799

Love Birds

Worked on pale pink fabric, this pretty pair of love birds nestling against a heart can be stitched for any love-themed occasion.

Stitch count 40h x 32w
Design size 7.3 x 5.8cm (2⅞ x 2¼in)

You will need

17.8 x 15.2cm (7 x 6in) 14-count pale pink Aida (DMC 818) ★
Size 26 tapestry needle ★
DMC threads as listed in chart key ★

For the stitching, use two strands for full and three-quarter cross stitch and for French knots and one strand for backstitch. See pages 98–99 if necessary.

To finish, mount the fabric in a double-fold card with a circular aperture. Place a heart-shaped brad through the fabric.

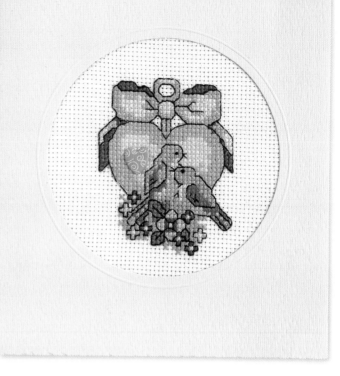

Valentine Cupid

This Cupid design with patterned papers and romantic embellishments is perfect for sending love on Valentine's Day.

Stitch count 54h x 37w
Design size 9.8 x 6.7cm (3⅞ x 2⅝in)

You will need

★ 20.3 x 17.8cm (8 x 7in) 14-count white Aida
★ Size 26 tapestry needle
★ DMC threads as listed in chart key

For the stitching, use two strands for full and three-quarter cross stitch and for French knots and one strand for backstitch. See pages 98–99 if necessary.

To finish, trim the fabric with pinking shears. Cover a single-fold base card with coloured card and patterned papers and a strip of patterned paper to cover the join. Stick the fabric on top using double-sided tape. Place three heart-themed circular stickers (DCWV) down the left-hand side.

Missing You

Send this cute teddy to let someone know they are in your thoughts. Pretty gingham papers echo areas of the stitched design.

Stitch count 54h x 44w
Design size 9.8 x 8cm (3⅞ x 3⅛in)

You will need

20.3 x 17.8cm (8 x 7in) 14-count white Aida ★
Size 26 tapestry needle ★
DMC threads as listed in chart key ★

For the stitching, use two strands for full and three-quarter cross stitch and one strand for backstitch. See pages 98–99 if necessary.

To finish, back the fabric with iron-on interfacing and trim. Layer the fabric on to patterned paper. Trim the right-hand edge of the front of the card and stick a strip of the same patterned paper on the inside of the card to show through from the front.

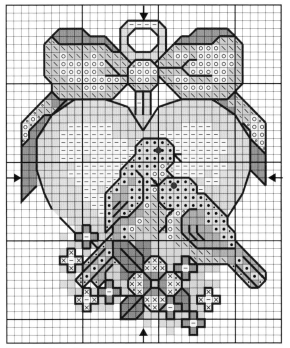

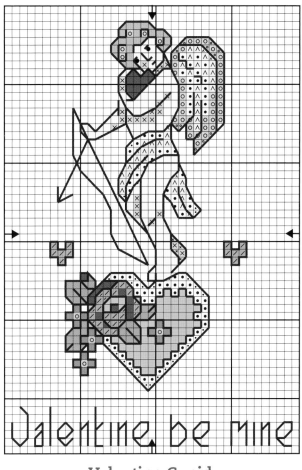

Love Birds

DMC stranded cotton
Cross stitch

Backstitch

▨	164	▨	676	⊙	818	▨	3839
✕	211	▨	702	╲	3716	•	3840
▨	553	−	745	▨	3831		

— 801

French knots

● 801

Valentine, be mine

Valentine Cupid

DMC stranded cotton
Cross stitch

Backstitch

▨	155	▨	948	
▨	309	╱	956	
✕	353	▨	977	
⊙	676	▨	3708	
∧	745	•	B5200	
▨	906			

— 3031

French knots

● 3031

Missing You

DMC stranded cotton
Cross stitch

Backstitch

−	168	∨	603	╱	3756	
⊙	341	▨	963	•	B5200	
▨	414	▨	3747			

— 414

Missing you

New Horizons

Sending a card to celebrate a memorable event or a great achievement is a wonderful way to let someone know you care. A hand-stitched card shows that you have spent the extra time and effort to let that special person know just how much you appreciate them.

There are always achievements worth celebrating, such as graduating, starting a new job or passing a driving test and a card is the perfect way to say 'Well Done'. Life-changing events are also celebrated in this chapter, and your good luck wishes will be much appreciated by friends and family who may be facing new horizons, such as moving home, emigrating or retiring.

Make it special. . .

Hand-crafted cards are always appreciated and even more so if you have taken the trouble to decorate the card mount too. Bright, patterned papers, brads and special themed embellishments can be used to complement your stitching and items such as lucky horseshoes, four-leaved clovers, transport motifs and peel-off stickers are usually very easy to find.

New Home

This charming card would be perfect for someone moving house. Memory thread was used to create pretty flower embellishments, which are held in place with tiny couching stitches. Thin coloured wire can be used in the same way.

Stitch count 65h x 51w
Design size 11.8 x 9.2cm (4⅝ x 3⅝in)

You will need

20 x 15cm (8 x 6in) 14-count white Aida ★
Size 26 tapestry needle ★
DMC threads as listed in chart key ★
DMC Desire memory thread or thin wire ★

For the stitching, use two strands for cross stitch and one strand for backstitch. Work the clouds in half cross stitch. See pages 98–99 if necessary.

To finish, trim the fabric with pinking shears and layer on to patterned papers using double-sided tape. Cover the front of a blue single-fold card with patterned papers. Shape the DMC Desire thread into simple flower patterns and stitch on to the fabric.

Retirement

This pretty retirement card has been decorated with button embellishments that reflect the floral theme. It would also make a lovely birthday card if the wording was changed.

Stitch count 39h x 59w
Design size 7 x 10.7cm (2¾ x 4¼in)

You will need

★ 14 x 18cm (5½ x 7in) 14-count mint green Aida (DMC 964)
★ Size 26 tapestry needle
★ DMC threads as listed in chart key

For the stitching, use two strands for cross stitch and one strand for backstitch. See pages 98–99 if necessary.

To finish, trim the fabric with pinking shears. Stitch buttons (Dovecraft) on to the fabric and then layer it on to patterned paper. Attach brads to the top corners. Cover a single-fold lemon card with patterned paper, and stick the layered fabric on top at an angle using double-sided tape.

New Home

DMC stranded cotton
Cross stitch

v	164		912
•	211	O	955
	341		963
╱	604		964
	722	□	3761
╲	726	✕	3855
	744	+	3856
	772		

Half cross stitch

I	3761

Backstitch
— 413

Retirement

DMC stranded cotton
Cross stitch

	155	v	745
	164		760
	168		911
O	211		3826
I	318	╱	3827
	351	✕	3840
╲	704	•	B5200
	726		

Backstitch
— 413

Driving Test

Passing a driving test is a great achievement, so make this fun card for a friend or family member to mark the occasion.

Stitch count 48h x 51w
Design size 8.7 x 9.2cm (3½ x 3⅝ in)

You will need

18 x 20cm (7 x 8in) 14-count white Aida ★
Size 26 tapestry needle ★
DMC threads as listed in chart key ★

For the stitching, use two strands for full and three-quarter cross stitch and one strand for backstitch. See pages 98–99 if necessary.

To finish, trim the fabric using pinking shears and layer on to yellow card using double-sided tape before layering again on to a single-fold white square card.

New Job

A pen embellishment sticker decorates this quick-to-stitch card. You could change the colour of the base card for a more feminine look.

Stitch count 19h x 19w (max for each motif)
Design size 3.4 x 3.4cm (1⅜ x 1⅜ in) (each motif)

You will need

★ Three 9 x 9cm (3½ x 3½in) squares of 14-count Aida (I used pale blue, yellow and green, DMC 964, 744, and 772)
★ Size 26 tapestry needle
★ DMC threads as listed in chart key

For the stitching, use two strands for full and three-quarter cross stitch and one strand for backstitch. See pages 98–99 if necessary.

To finish, back the fabric with iron-on interfacing and trim before sticking on to squares of white card using double-sided tape. Stick a strip of striped paper down the left side of a tall blue single-fold card. Attach the layered fabric to the card and add a pen embellishment (Artoz-Artwork).

Graduation

This fun card is suitable for any exam subject. A girl's face is also charted so that the card can be stitched for either gender.

Stitch count 52h x 30w
Design size 9.4 x 5.4cm (3¾ x 2⅛ in)

You will need

16 x 12cm (6¼ x 4¾in) 14-count white Aida ★
Size 26 tapestry needle ★
DMC threads as listed in chart key ★

For the stitching, use two strands for full and three-quarter cross stitch and one strand for French knots and for backstitch. See pages 98–99 if necessary. Follow the instructions with the chart for stitching a girl's face.

To finish, back the fabric with iron-on interfacing and trim before layering on to red and yellow card using double-sided tape. Cover a single-fold rectangular card with patterned chalk-board paper and stick the layered fabric on top.

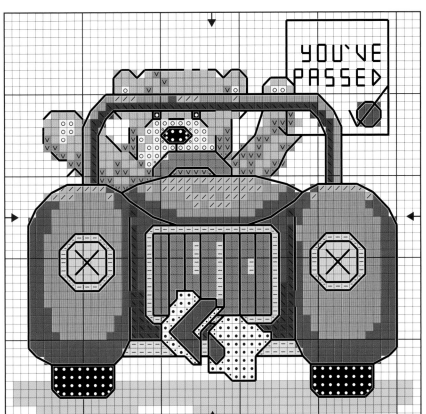

Driving Test

DMC stranded cotton
Cross stitch

●	310	◣	498
	351		666
╱	352		703
	414	O	712
─	415		726
V	435	●	blanc
	437		

Backstitch
— 310

To change the graduation chart to female, replace the stitches within the red dashed box

New Job

DMC stranded cotton
Cross stitch

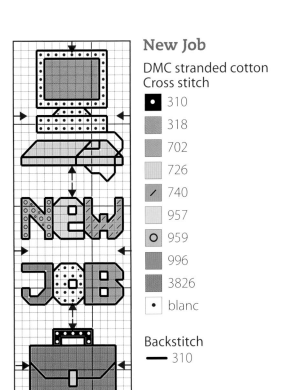

●	310
	318
	702
	726
╱	740
	957
O	959
	996
	3826
●	blanc

Backstitch
— 310

Graduation

DMC stranded
cotton
Cross stitch

●	310
╱	413
	666
	701
	744
	798
	818
	3716
●	blanc

Backstitch
— 310

French knots
● 310

Good Luck

A lucky horseshoe and a four-leaf clover embellish this bright card, which would be suitable for many occasions. Areas of DMC Light Effects thread add a metallic look.

Stitch count 34h x 34w
Design size 6.2 x 6.2cm (2½ x 2½in)

You will need
12 x 12cm (5 x 5in) 14-count white Aida ★
Size 26 tapestry needle ★
DMC threads as listed in chart key ★

For the stitching, use two strands for full and three-quarter cross stitch and for French knots and one strand for backstitch. See pages 98–99 if necessary.

To finish, back the fabric with iron-on interfacing and layer on to red card using double-sided tape. Stick the layered fabric on to a single-fold green card and decorate with a strip of yellow card, brads and lucky charm embellishments (Dovecraft).

Well Done

This colourful card will suit various occasions where congratulations are in order. A foam champagne bottle sticker complements the theme.

Stitch count 31h x 31w
Design size 5.6 x 5.6cm (2¼ x 2¼in)

You will need
★ 12 x 12cm (5 x 5in) 14-count white Aida
★ Size 26 tapestry needle
★ DMC threads as listed in chart key

For the stitching, use two strands for full and three-quarter cross stitch and one strand for backstitch. See pages 98–99 if necessary.

To finish, mount the fabric in a yellow double-fold card with a square aperture. Decorate the front of the card with patterned paper and foam embellishments (Dovecraft).

Bon Voyage

Bold motifs create this travel-themed card, perfect for anyone leaving on a voyage. Change the wording to 'Good Luck', to make the card suitable to give to someone emigrating.

Stitch count 45h x 46w
Design size 8.3 x 8.3cm (3¼ x 3¼in)

You will need
16 x 16cm (6¼ x 6¼in) 14-count white Aida ★
Size 26 tapestry needle ★
DMC threads as listed in chart key ★

For the stitching, use two strands for cross stitch and one strand for backstitch. See pages 98–99 if necessary.

To finish, mount the fabric within a blue double-fold card with a square aperture. Glue striped and gingham paper across the bottom of the front of the card, then cut to follow the aperture shape.

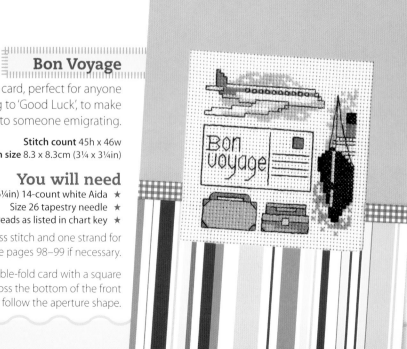

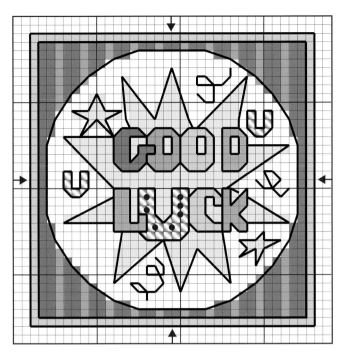

Good Luck

DMC stranded cotton
Cross stitch

▨ 666	▨ 740	
▨ 703	▨ 996	
▨ 726	▨ E415 (Light Effects)	

Backstitch

— 310

French knots

● 310

Well Done

DMC stranded cotton
Cross stitch

▨ 318	▨ 666	⊙ 740
▨ 415	▨ 702	▨ 798
▨ 435	▨ 726	• B5200

Backstitch

— 310

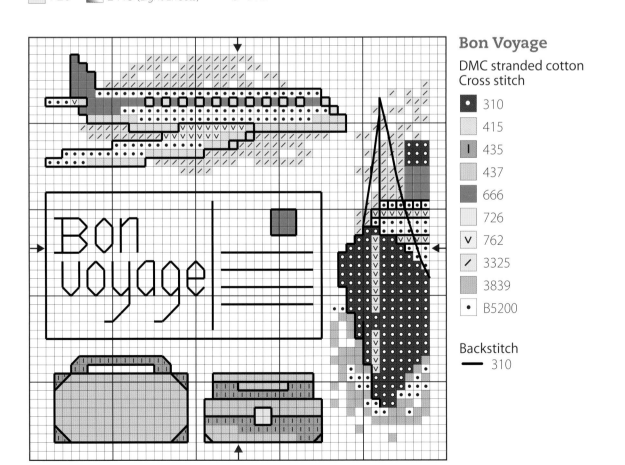

Bon Voyage

DMC stranded cotton
Cross stitch

▨ •	310
▨	415
I	435
▨	437
▨	666
▨	726
v	762
╱	3325
▨	3839
•	B5200

Backstitch

— 310

Calendar Events

There are many seasonal events that are celebrated once a year and this next chapter is filled with all sorts of lovely card designs perfect for those occasions. For example, in spring we celebrate Easter and St Patrick's Day; in summer there is American Independence Day and in the fall, amid warm autumnal colours, we remember Hallowe'en and Thanksgiving. Card ideas for winter and the festive season are provided in the section beginning on page 80.

This chapter also includes three traditional sampler cards to celebrate spring, summer and autumn. The winter sampler card can be found on pages 86–87 and all four could be stitched as a set (see picture opposite title page) or framed as charming little pictures.

Make it special...

Craft shops and online stores are filled with a fabulous selection of seasonal embellishments and you will find plenty of inspiration for once-a-year celebrations. Let the predominant colours of each season influence your choice of embellishments; for example, choose sugary pastels for spring, bright floral colours for summer and rich reds and golds for autumn.

Happy Easter

A delightful bunny adorns this Easter card. The background sky is stitched in half cross stitch and pretty embellishments complete the Easter theme.

Stitch count 48h x 48w
Design size 8.7 x 8.7cm (3½ x 3½in)

You will need

★ 18 x 18cm (7 x 7in) 14-count white Aida
★ Size 26 tapestry needle
★ DMC threads as listed in chart key

For the stitching, use two strands for full and three-quarter cross stitch and the single French knot and one strand for backstitch. Work the sky in half cross stitch. See pages 98–99 if necessary.

To finish, mount the card within a pale green double-fold card with a square aperture. Decorate the card with Easter embellishment stickers (Dovecraft) and a ribbon bow.

St Patrick's Day

St Patrick's Day is the national holiday of Ireland, usually celebrated on 17 March. This design has been stitched using the traditional green.

Stitch count 41h x 41w
Design size 7.5 x 7.5cm (3 x 3in)

You will need

15 x 15cm (6 x 6in) 14-count white Aida ★
Size 26 tapestry needle ★
DMC threads as listed in chart key ★

For the stitching, use two strands for full and three-quarter cross stitch and one strand for backstitch. See pages 98–99 if necessary.

To finish, back the fabric with iron-on interfacing and layer on to yellow card. Secure brads in each of the four corners and layer on to a bright green single-fold square card.

Spring Sampler

This delightful mini sampler card is a great way to celebrate spring and would also make a charming little framed picture. There are designs for summer, autumn and winter on pages 76, 78 and 86.

Stitch count 58h x 39w
Design size 10.5 x 7cm (4⅛ x 2¾in)

You will need

★ 20 x 16cm (8 x 6¼in) 14-count white Aida
★ Size 26 tapestry needle
★ DMC threads as listed in chart key

For the stitching, use two strands for cross stitch and one strand for backstitch. See pages 98–99 if necessary.

To finish, trim the fabric with pinking shears and then layer on to coloured card using double-sided tape. Secure brads in each corner and stick on to a pink single-fold base card.

Happy Easter

DMC stranded cotton
Cross stitch

V	164		726	O	957		3832
\	168	I	745		963		3838
X	209		911	—	964	•	blanc
/	211		955		3746		

Half cross stitch

	519

Backstitch   **French knot**
— 413   ● 413

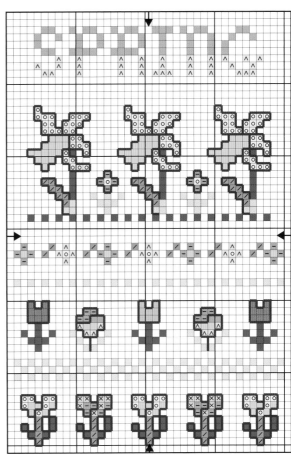

St Patrick's Day

DMC stranded cotton
Cross stitch

						Backstitch
	208	/	702		740	— 310
O	666		704		796	
	699		726		996	

Spring Sampler

DMC stranded cotton
Cross stitch

								Backstitch
^	153		209		743		3350	— 319
—	155		699	O	745	X	3840	— 898
	164	/	702		957			

4th July

Celebrate 4th July in style with this bold card in traditional red, blue and white. Tiny stars punched from paper decorate the base card.

Stitch count 64h x 27w
Design size 11.6 x 5cm (4½ x 2in)

You will need

18 x 12cm (7 x 4¾in) 14-count white Aida ★
Size 26 tapestry needle ★
DMC threads as listed in chart key ★

For the stitching, use two strands for full and three-quarter cross stitch and one strand for backstitch. See pages 98–99 if necessary.

To finish, trim the fabric with pinking shears. Cut a mount from red card and layer over the top. Cover the single-fold base card with gingham-patterned paper and add a border of punched stars to a striped border. Stick the fabric on top using double-sided tape.

Summer Sampler

This pretty summer-themed card is the second in a set of four designs. You could stitch all four together as a larger, framed sampler.

Stitch count 59h x 39w
Design size 10.7 x 7cm (4¼ x 2¾in)

You will need

★ 20 x 16cm (8 x 6¼in) 14-count white Aida
★ Size 26 tapestry needle
★ DMC threads as listed in chart key

For the stitching, use two strands for cross stitch and one strand for backstitch. See pages 98–99 if necessary.

To finish, trim the fabric with pinking shears and layer on to coloured card using double-sided tape. Secure brads in each corner before sticking on to a single-fold base card.

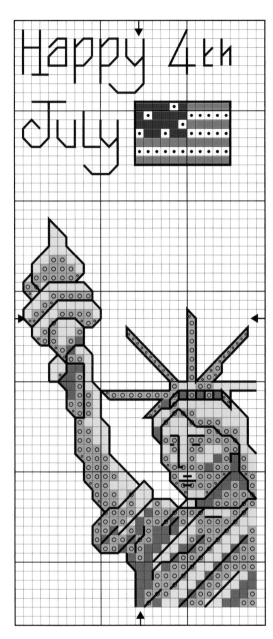

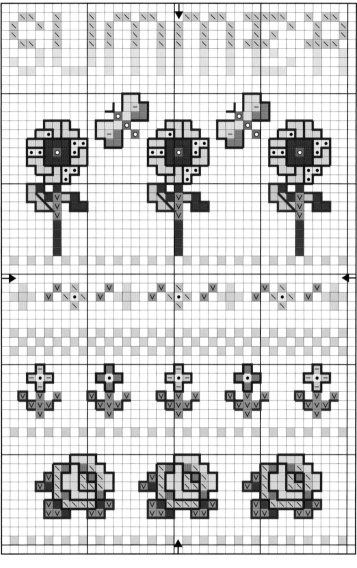

4th July

DMC stranded cotton
Cross stitch

			Backstitch
▨	666	▨ 3811	— 310
▨	796	O 3849	
▨	3809	• blanc	

Summer Sampler

DMC stranded cotton
Cross stitch

						Backstitch
▨ 164	v 702	▨ 898	▨ 3350			— 319
⊙ 434	▨ 743	＼ 957	▨ 3838			— 898
▨ 699	• 745	▨ 963	— 3840			

Hallowe'en

This eye-catching Hallowe'en card could be stitched as a seasonal party invitation or to celebrate someone's birthday at that time of year.

Stitch count 44h x 43w
Design size 8 x 7.8cm (3⅛ x 3in)

You will need

★ 16 x 16cm (6¼ x 6¼in) 14-count white Aida
★ Size 26 tapestry needle
★ DMC threads as listed in chart key

For the stitching, use two strands for full and three-quarter cross stitch and French knots and one strand for backstitch. See pages 98–99 if necessary.

To finish, trim the fabric with pinking shears and layer on to purple card using double-sided tape. Decorate the bottom of a black single-fold card with a length of printed twill. Stick squares of white and orange card above and fasten black brads to each corner of the orange card. Stick the layered fabric on top at an angle.

Thanksgiving

This traditional themed card is decorated with patterned paper in autumnal colours and completed with a paper flower embellishment.

Stitch count 42h x 42w
Design size 7.6 x 7.6cm (3 x 3in)

You will need

16 x 16cm (6¼ x 6¼in) 14-count white Aida ★
Size 26 tapestry needle ★
DMC threads as listed in chart key ★

For the stitching, use two strands for full and three-quarter cross stitch and one strand for backstitch. See pages 98–99 if necessary.

To finish, mount the fabric in double-fold card with a square aperture. Glue patterned paper and a flower embellishment (Chatterbox) on to the front of the base card following the shape of the aperture, trimming as necessary.

Autumn Sampler

This card is the third in the set of mini seasonal sampler cards and celebrates autumn, that season of mists and mellow fruitfulness.

Stitch count 57h x 39w
Design size 10.2 x 7cm (4 x 2¾in)

You will need

★ 20 x 16cm (8 x 6¼in) 14-count white Aida
★ Size 26 tapestry needle
★ DMC threads as listed in chart key

For the stitching, use two strands for full and three-quarter cross stitch and one strand for backstitch. See pages 98–99 if necessary.

To finish, trim the fabric with pinking shears and then layer on to coloured card using double-sided tape. Secure brads in each corner before sticking on to a red single-fold base card.

Hallowe'en

DMC stranded cotton
Cross stitch

\	208	∧	436		726	948
	211		550		740	
⊙	310		700		742	
	433		703	✕	946	

Backstitch   French knots
—— 310   ● 310

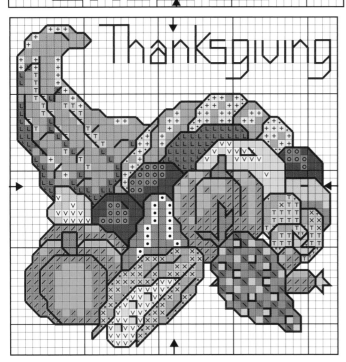

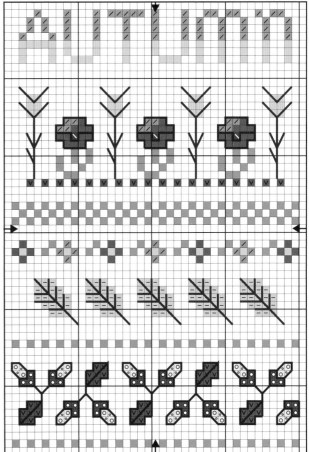

Thanksgiving

DMC stranded cotton
Cross stitch   Backstitch

\	208	L	434		741		3348	——	310
	209		437	v	745	T	3827		
	211	✕	676	•	746				
	347		726	/	947				
⊙	351	+	738		3347				

Autumn Sampler

DMC stranded cotton
Cross stitch   Backstitch

\	319	v	699		743	——	319	
•	434		702	O	745	——	898	
	666	/	740	–	3827			

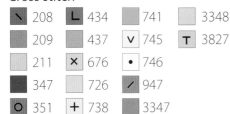

Cards for Christmas

Cards and Christmas time go together like a sleigh ride and snow. Hand-stitched cards are great fun to create and are sure to stand out from the rest of the shop-bought greetings that sit on our mantelpieces during the festive season. Colour schemes can be varied too, not just teaming the traditional red and green but silver and blue or mulberry and gold.

In this chapter you will find a great range of attractive cards, from cute and fun to contemporary and traditional. It is easy to personalize a card for a family member or a friend by adding simple stitched text using one of the backstitch charts provided on pages 37, 45, 61 and 92.

Make it special. . .

Christmas embellishments are available in many colourways – from traditional red, gold and green to contemporary silver, pink and aqua – so you are sure to find an array of festive goodies to suit your projects. It is tempting to go over the top and add too many finishing touches, but with most projects it is nearly always the case of 'less is more'.

Christmas Angel

To give this traditionally themed design a contemporary twist, blue and silver embellishments were used to finish off the card. DMC Light Effects thread adds a golden gleam to the stitching.

Stitch count 37h x 39w
Design size 6.7 x 7cm (2⅝ x 2¾in)

You will need

★ 15.2 x 15.2cm (6 x 6in) 14-count iridescent Aida (DMC DC27D)
★ Size 26 tapestry needle
★ DMC threads as listed in chart key

For the stitching, use two strands for full and three-quarter cross stitch and one strand for backstitch. See pages 98–99 if necessary.

To finish, back the fabric with iron-on interfacing, trim and stick to silver card with double-sided tape. Stick this on to a blue single-fold card and decorate with snowflake stickers and a band of patterned paper (DCWV). Place silver peel-off stickers on the right-hand corner and stick a metal charm (Making Memories) on the left-hand side.

Tinsel Cat

This fun design of a mischievous cat is complemented by bright and bold patterned papers. DMC Light Effects thread gives the tinsel extra sparkle.

Stitch count 37h x 24w
Design size 6.7 x 4.5cm (2⅝ x 1¾in)

You will need

15.2 x 12.7cm (6 x 5in) 14-count white Aida ★
Size 26 tapestry needle ★
DMC threads as listed in chart key ★

For the stitching, use two strands for full and three-quarter cross stitch and one strand for backstitch. See pages 98–99 if necessary.

To finish, back the fabric with iron-on interfacing, trim and layer on to blue card using double-sided tape. Stick a strip of patterned paper (Dovecraft) across the bottom of a white single-fold card. Attach a rectangle of coordinating paper on to the card at an angle and stick the layered fabric on top.

Robin's Stocking

Brightly coloured patterned papers are used to complement this cheery robin design.

Stitch count 40h x 38w
Design size 7.3 x 7cm (2⅞ x 2¾in)

You will need

★ 15.2 x 12.7cm (6 x 5in) 14-count white Aida
★ Size 26 tapestry needle
★ DMC threads as listed in chart key

For the stitching, use two strands for full and three-quarter cross stitch and one strand for backstitch. See pages 98–99 if necessary.

To finish, back the fabric with iron-on interfacing, trim and layer on to red card using double-sided tape. Decorate a single-fold card with patterned paper (Dovecraft) and stick the layered fabric on top. Attach 'let it snow', cut from a sheet of coordinating paper, below the fabric.

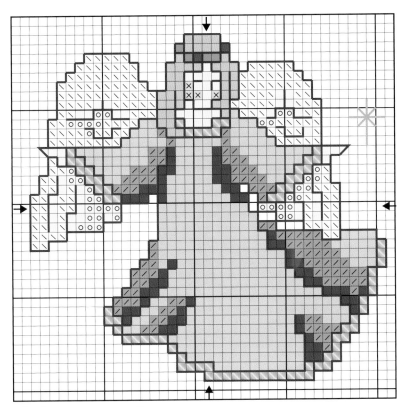

Christmas Angel

DMC stranded cotton
Cross stitch

▨ 162	▨ 676	☐ 948	◹ B5200
▨ 349	○ 746	✕ 963	▨ E3821 (Light Effects)
◹ 519	▨ 911	▨ 3760	

Backstitch
— 3799
— E3821

Tinsel Cat

DMC stranded cotton
Cross stitch

				Backstitch
☐ 415	▨ 738			— 310
◹ 436	▨ 995			
⊡ 498	○ 3716			
▨ 666	◹ B5200			
I 702	▨ E3821 (Light Effects)			

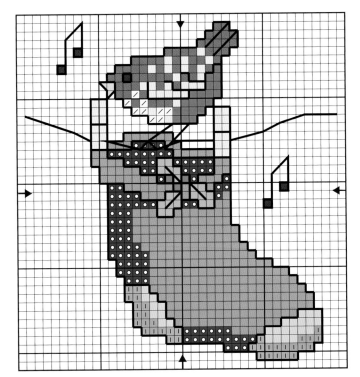

Robin's Stocking

DMC stranded cotton
Cross stitch

		Backstitch
▨ 310	▨ 726	— 310
▨ 434	☐ 738	
▨ 666	I 741	
▨ 703	⊡ 995	
◹ 712	▨ 996	

Skating Penguins

For this fun design, the front right-hand side of the card was cut away for a 3D effect, giving the appearance of motion to the penguins.

Stitch count 34h x 52w
Design size 6.2 x 9.4cm (2½ x 3¾in)

You will need

15.2 x 17.8cm (6 x 7in) 14-count white Aida ★
Size 26 tapestry needle ★
DMC threads as listed in chart key ★

For the stitching, use two strands for cross stitch and one strand for backstitch. See pages 98–99 if necessary.

To finish, back the fabric with iron-on interfacing, trim and layer on to patterned paper (Pebbles Inc) using double-sided tape. Cut away the front right-hand side of the base card. Cover the front with coordinating paper and stick contrasting paper on the inside. Stick a striped piece of paper across the bottom inside and front and place stickers on the striped paper. Stick the layered stitching on to the front of the card, allowing it to overhang the right-hand side.

Santa's Sleigh

A traditional Santa card has been finished off using fun papers and embellishments.

Stitch count 33h x 45w
Design size 6 x 8.2cm (2⅜ x 3¼in)

You will need

★ 15.2 x 15.2cm (6 x 6in) 14-count Aida
★ Size 26 tapestry needle
★ DMC threads as listed in chart key

For the stitching, use two strands for full and three-quarter cross stitch and for the French knot and one for backstitch. See pages 98–99 if necessary.

To finish, back the fabric with iron-on interfacing, trim and layer on to red card and then patterned paper (Doodlebug) using double-sided tape. Cover the front of a rectangular single-fold card using pieces of coordinating paper and ribbon. Stick the layered fabric on the right side of the card and place the embellishments (Doodlebug) down the left side. Place a 'traditions' sticker on the right-hand side of the ribbon.

Carolling Mouse

The theme of a singing mouse has been reflected in the jingle bells embellishment. The tall base card and simple layering give a modern twist.

Stitch count 37h x 26w
Design size 6.7 x 4.7cm (2⅝ x 1⅞in)

You will need

15.2 x 12.7cm (6 x 5in) 14-count white Aida ★
Size 26 tapestry needle ★
DMC threads as listed in chart key ★

For the stitching, use two strands for cross stitch and one strand for backstitch. See pages 98–99 if necessary.

To finish, back the fabric with iron-on interfacing, trim and layer on to a strip of yellow card using double-sided tape. Tear the bottom of the card to reveal a white chamfered edge. Place a 'Jingle all the way' sticker (Dovecraft) at the top, then stick the layered card on to a tall, red single-fold card.

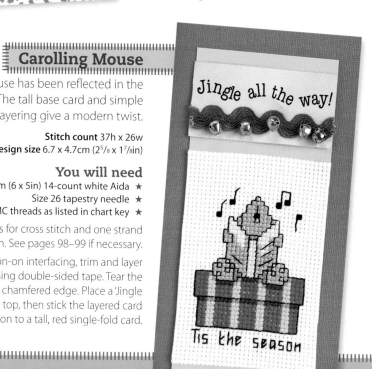

Skating Penguins

DMC stranded cotton
Cross stitch

•	310		701
	413		726
I	415	O	741
\	498	V	747
	519	/	B5200
	666		

Backstitch
— 310

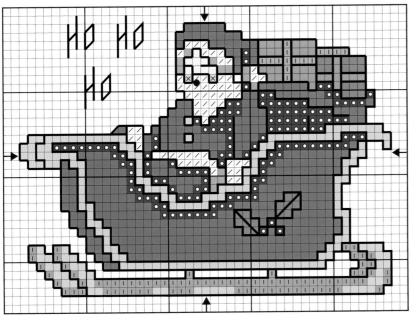

Ho Ho
Ho

Santa's Sleigh

DMC stranded cotton
Cross stitch

		Backstitch
	415	I 740	— 310

	415	I	740
•	498		948
	666	×	963
	702	/	996
	726	/	blanc

Backstitch
— 310

French knot
● 310

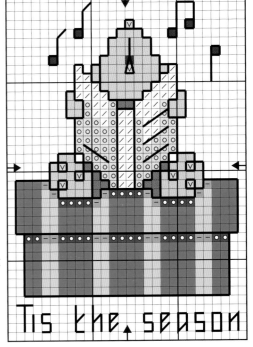

Carolling Mouse

DMC stranded cotton
Cross stitch

O	168	V	605		738
	310		666	—	741
	436		726	/	blanc
•	498				

Backstitch
— 310

Tis the season

Snowy Scene

This lovely winter scene was stitched on sparkling iridescent Aida to enhance the look of sunrise on soft snow.

Stitch count 37h x 64w
Design size 6.7 x 11.6cm (2⅝ x 4½in)

You will need

★ 15.2 x 19cm (6 x 7½in) 14-count white iridescent Aida (DMC DC27D)
★ Size 26 tapestry needle
★ DMC threads as listed in chart key

For the stitching, use two strands for full and three-quarter cross stitch and one strand for backstitch. See pages 98–99 if necessary.

To finish, trim the fabric within an oval aperture card. Stick a strip of patterned paper (K&Co) across the bottom. Place a tree and 'Noel' sticker (K&Co) on to the bottom left of the aperture to lie partly on the fabric.

Winter Sampler

This winter-themed card is the last in the set of charming seasonal sampler cards – see page 74 for spring, page 76 for summer and page 78 for autumn.

Stitch count 58h x 40w
Design size 10.5 x 7.3cm (4⅛ x 2⅞in)

You will need

17.8 x 15.2cm (7 x 6in) 14-count white Aida ★
Size 26 tapestry needle ★
DMC threads as listed in chart key ★

For the stitching, use two strands for cross stitch and one strand for backstitch. See pages 98–99 if necessary.

To finish, trim the fabric with pinking shears and then layer on to coloured card using double-sided tape. Secure brads in each corner before sticking on to a single-fold base card.

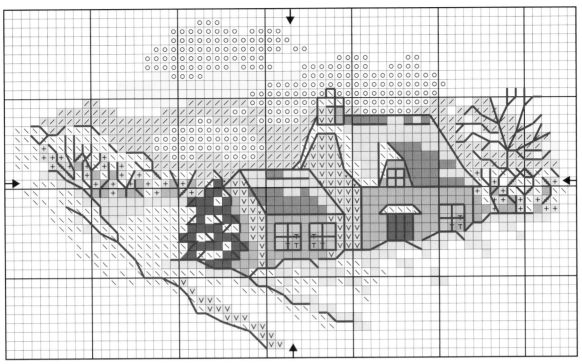

Snowy Scene

DMC stranded cotton
Cross stitch

	318	T	741
+	415	/	744
	435		745
	437	O	746
	505		775
	725		932
V	739	\	B5200

Backstitch
— 3799

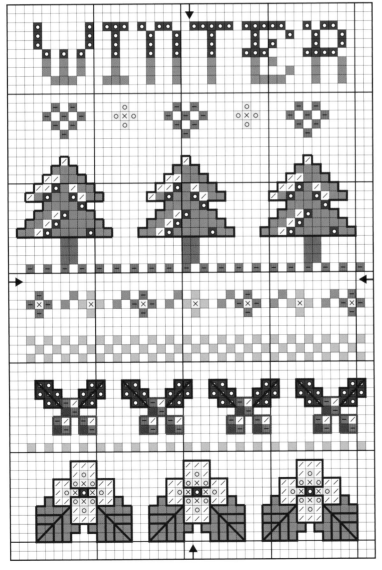

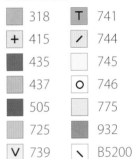

Winter Sampler

DMC stranded cotton
Cross stitch

	150		702	–	3350
	434	×	745		3733
●	699	O	963	/	blanc

Backstitch
— 319
— 898

Last-minute Greetings

The small motifs in this chapter are ideal for making gift tags for special presents, as shown opposite. These quick-to-stitch designs are also perfect for making last-minute greetings cards when you want to send your congratulations immediately the news is heard; for example, on learning that a friend is expecting a baby.

I hope that the selection of cards featured in this chapter will inspire you to combine your stitching and papercrafting skills to create hand-crafted greetings even when time is short. The finished design sizes given throughout the chapter are based on stitching the designs on 14-count Aida. For all designs, use two strands of thread for full and three-quarter cross stitches, two strands for French knots and one strand for backstitches.

Make it special...

When creating smaller cards and tags take care to choose embellishments that will be in scale with smaller motifs to avoid overpowering the cross stitch. Keeping things simple will stop them from looking too fussy. If cards and tags are needed in a hurry it is a good idea to store a collection of decorative elements so you can quickly find suitable embellishments.

drib-ble v. 1. Moving the ball down the field with short rapid kicks 2. What parents do with their drinks when their kid misses a goal

Belated Birthday

This jolly little card could also be used for a punctual birthday by not stitching the word 'Belated'. The balloons or cake could be stitched as separate motifs to make up little tags.

Stitch count 35h x 24w
Design size 6.4 x 4.4cm (2½ x 1¾in)

You will need
★ 15.2 x 12.7cm (6 x 5in) 14-count white Aida
★ Size 26 tapestry needle
★ DMC threads as listed in chart key

For the stitching, use two strands for cross stitch and one strand for backstitch. See pages 98–99 if necessary.

To finish, back the fabric with iron-on interfacing, trim and layer on to dark blue card. Decorate the front of a single-fold card with patterned papers (Dovecraft) and ribbon. Stick the layered fabric on to the left-hand side and add a birthday-themed sticker (Provo Craft) on the right-hand side.

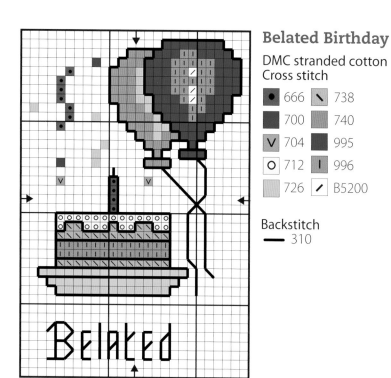

Belated Birthday

DMC stranded cotton
Cross stitch

●	666	◣	738
	700		740
V	704		995
O	712	I	996
	726	◪	B5200

Backstitch
— 310

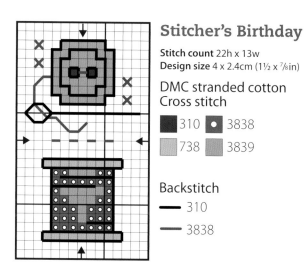

Stitcher's Birthday

Stitch count 22h x 13w
Design size 4 x 2.4cm (1½ x ⅞in)

DMC stranded cotton
Cross stitch

	310	○	3838
	738		3839

Backstitch
— 310
— 3838

A card using this design is shown on page 101

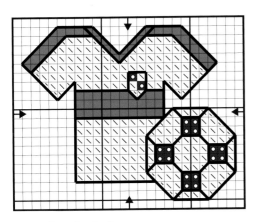

Men's Birthday

Stitch count 19h x 24w
Design size 3.4 x 4.4cm (1⅜ x 1¾in)

DMC stranded cotton
Cross stitch

⬛ 310   🟥 666   ◣ B5200

Backstitch
—— 310

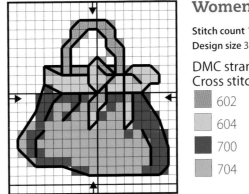

Women's Birthday

Stitch count 17h x 17w
Design size 3cm (1¼in) square

DMC stranded cotton
Cross stitch   Backstitch

🟪 602   —— 310
⬜ 604
⬛ 700
🟪 704

Thank You

The motif may be small but the card says a big thank you. The mounting is simple so the card can be made very quickly.

Stitch count 15h x 12w
Design size 2.7 x 2.2cm (1 x ⅞in)

You will need

10.2 x 10.2cm (4 x 4in) 14-count white Aida ★
Size 26 tapestry needle ★
DMC threads as listed in chart key ★

For the stitching, use two strands for cross stitch and one strand for backstitch. See pages 98–99 if necessary.

To finish, mount the fabric on a square aperture double-fold card that has been covered with patterned paper (MOD). Cut gingham-printed paper into a strip to resemble ribbon, attach to the card and add a sticker (K&Co) for the finishing touch.

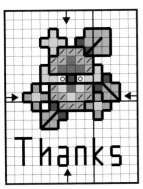

Thank You

DMC stranded cotton
Cross stitch

🟪 602   ⭕ 712
⬜ 604   🟨 726
⬛ 700   🟪 3838
🟪 704   ◤ 3839

Backstitch   —— 310

This simple motif is teamed with attractive patterned paper, making an elegant statement. The stitching could also be layered on to card and stuck on to a single-fold card.

Stitch count 21h x 25w
Design size 3.8 x 4.5cm (1½ x 1¾in)

You will need
★ 12.7 x 12.7cm (5 x 5in) 14-count white Aida
★ Size 26 tapestry needle
★ DMC threads as listed in chart key

For the stitching, use two strands for cross stitch and one strand for backstitch. See pages 98–99 if necessary.

Cover a square aperture double-fold card with patterned scrapbook paper (Sandylion) and mount the cross stitch in the card. Attach an adhesive gem (Papermania) on to the stitched diamond.

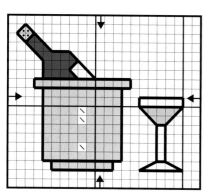

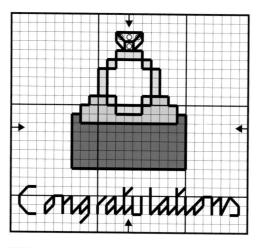

Engagement

DMC stranded cotton
Cross stitch

	604
	676
	3838
O	B5200

Backstitch
— 310

Congratulations

Stitch count 16h x 19w
Design size 2.9 x 3.4cm (1⅛ x 1⅜in)

DMC stranded cotton
Cross stitch

	168		726
●	676	\	B5200
	700		

Backstitch
— 310

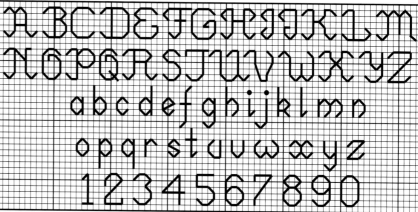

Use this backstitch chart to personalize the designs

Wedding Invitation

This motif is so quick to stitch that it would be ideal for producing lots of wedding invitation cards. It could also be used on place name cards for the wedding table. If desired, guests' names could be added using the alphabet on page 27 or opposite, creating the perfect keepsake.

Stitch count 22h x 12w
Design size 4 x 2.2cm (1½ x ⅞in)

You will need
11.5 x 10.2cm (4½ x 4in) 14-count white Aida ★
Size 26 tapestry needle ★
DMC threads as listed in chart key ★

For the stitching, use two strands for cross stitch and one strand for backstitch. See pages 98–99 if necessary.

To finish, back the fabric with iron-on interfacing, trim and layer on to a blue card tag. Cover the front of a single-fold base card with the same blue card and then layer patterned paper (K&Co) on top. Punch a heart from the bottom right-hand corner of the patterned paper and stick it to the front of the base card. Attach the tag on top and add a ring embellishment to the punched-out heart shape.

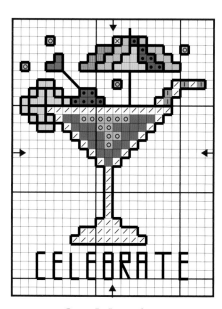

General Celebration

Stitch count 29h x 22w
Design size 5.3 x 4cm (2 x 1½in)

DMC stranded cotton
Cross stitch

▨ 602	▨ 726	⊙ 996
● 666	Ɩ 740	╱ B5200
▨ 700	✕ 963	**Backstitch**
▨ 704	▨ 995	— 310

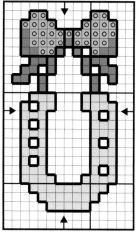

Wedding Invitation

DMC stranded cotton
Cross stitch   Backstitch

▨ 168	⊙ 3839	— 310
▨ 3838		

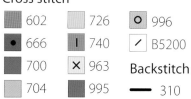

Congratulations, You're Expecting!

This motif has been made into a congratulations card for a mother-to-be, but it could also be used as a baby shower gift tag or a welcome baby card or tag.

Stitch count 20h x 15w
Design size 3.6 x 2.7cm (1⅜ x 1⅛in)

You will need

11.4 x 10.2cm (4½ x 4in) 14-count white Aida ★
Size 26 tapestry needle ★
DMC threads as listed in chart key ★

For the stitching, use two strands for cross stitch and one strand for backstitch. See pages 98–99 if necessary.

To finish, back the fabric with iron-on interfacing, trim and layer on to yellow card. Cover the front of a single-fold card with scrapbook paper (Sandylion). Stick on the layered fabric and add matching stickers to complete the card.

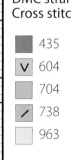

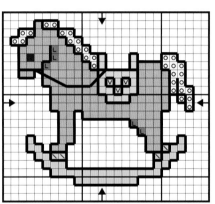

New Baby Boy

DMC stranded cotton
Cross stitch

⧵	168	O	712
V	211		726
■	310		738
L	435		955

Backstitch
— 310

Congratulations, You're Expecting!

DMC stranded cotton
Cross stitch

⧵	353		955
	604	V	963
O	712		3838
	726	—	3839

Backstitch — 413

New Baby Girl

Stitch count 32h x 22w
Design size 5.8 x 4cm (2¼ x 1½in)

DMC stranded cotton
Cross stitch

	435
V	604
	704
╱	738
	963

Backstitch
— 413

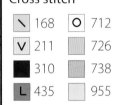

Good Luck

Whether it's a forthcoming exam, a driving test or a job interview, this stylish little card with its horseshoe motif will be the perfect way to send your support and best wishes.

Stitch count 18h x 10w
Design size 3.3 x 1.8cm (1¼ x ¾in)

You will need

11.4 x 10.2cm (4½ x 4in) 14-count white Aida ★
Size 26 tapestry needle ★
DMC threads as listed in chart key ★

For the stitching, use two strands for full and three-quarter cross stitch and French knots and one strand for backstitch. See pages 98–99 if necessary.

To finish, back the fabric with iron-on interfacing, trim and layer on to coloured card. Stick this on to the front of a green single-fold base card.

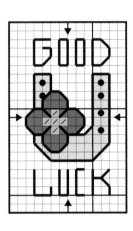

Good Luck

DMC stranded cotton

Cross stitch	Backstitch
168	— 310
700	
✕ 704	

French knots
● 310

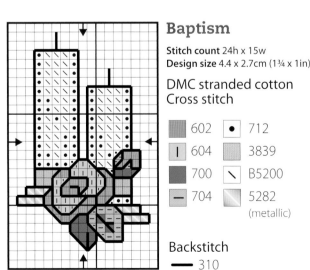

Baptism

Stitch count 24h x 15w
Design size 4.4 x 2.7cm (1¾ x 1in)

DMC stranded cotton
Cross stitch

602		•	712
I	604		3839
	700	╲	B5200
—	704		5282 (metallic)

Backstitch
— 310

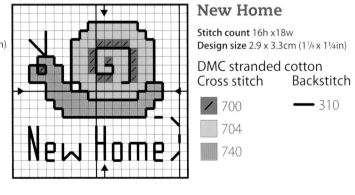

New Home

Stitch count 16h x18w
Design size 2.9 x 3.3cm (1⅛ x 1¼in)

DMC stranded cotton

Cross stitch	Backstitch
╱ 700	— 310
704	
740	

Get Well Soon

A band aid motif has been used to make this ultra quick-to-stitch get well card.

Stitch count 12h x 18w
Design size 2.2 x 3.3cm (⅞ x 1¼in)

You will need

10.2 x 11.4cm (4 x 4½in) 14-count white Aida ★
Size 26 tapestry needle ★
DMC threads as listed in chart key ★

For the stitching, use two strands for full and three-quarter cross stitch and French knots and one strand for backstitch. See pages 98–99 if necessary.

To finish, back the fabric with iron-on interfacing and layer on to coloured card. Cover the bottom half of an orange single-fold card with patterned paper (DCWV). Attach the layered fabric on to the card and add a metal charm (Making Memories) for decoration.

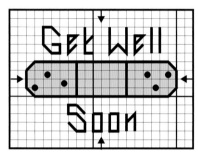

Get Well Soon

DMC stranded cotton
Cross stitch   Backstitch
[ ] 726   ── 310

French knots
● 310

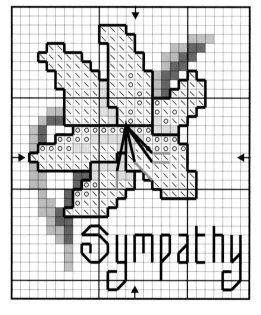

Sympathy

DMC stranded cotton
Cross stitch   Backstitch
[ ] 353   ── 310
[ ] 700   ─ ─ 740
[ ] 704
○ 712
\ B5200

Sympathy

Soft peachy pinks were used for this delicate card, with a little satin bow as the perfect finishing touch.

Stitch count 29h x 24w
Design size 5.3 x 4.3cm (2 x 1¾in)

You will need

★ 12.7 x 12.7cm (5 x 5in) 14-count white Aida
★ Size 26 tapestry needle
★ DMC threads as listed in chart key

For the stitching, use two strands for cross stitch and one strand for backstitch. See pages 98–99 if necessary.

To finish, back the fabric with iron-on interfacing, trim and layer on to patterned paper (Anna Griffin). Cover the front of a single-fold card with coordinating paper. Attach the layered fabric on to the card. Create a bow using satin ribbon and glue it to the front of the card below the patch.

Christmas

Here we have three quick-to-stitch Christmas motifs, which can be stitched singly and mounted to create speedy festive greetings. Alternatively, you could stitch all three motifs as patches and combine them with Christmas buttons or other embellishments, such as stickers, rub-ons or metallic charms.

You will need (for each stitched motif)
★ 12.7 x 12.7cm (5 x 5in) 14-count white Aida
★ Size 26 tapestry needle
★ DMC threads as listed in chart key

For the stitching, use two strands for cross stitch and one strand for backstitch. See pages 98–99 if necessary.

To finish the four-patch card, decorate a square single-fold base card with patterned papers. Back the four fabric patches with iron-on interfacing, trim and layer on to a square of patterned paper and stick this on to the base card. Add a Christmas embellishment (Doodlebug) to complete the card.

To finish the reindeer card, mount the fabric in a single-fold card with a square crinkle-cut aperture (Making Memories). Decorate the front of the card using coordinating ribbon, charms, stickers and rub-ons (Making Memories). To cover the reverse of the stitching, stick a rectangle of card on the inside of the card over the top of the fabric.

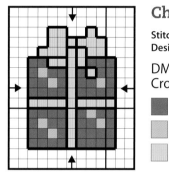

Christmas Present

Stitch count 12h x 9w
Design size 2.2 x 1.6cm (⅞ x ⅝in)

DMC stranded cotton

Cross stitch	Backstitch
■ 666	— 310
▨ 704	
▨ 726	

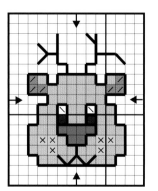

Christmas Reindeer

Stitch count 13h x 10w
Design size 2.4 x 1.8cm (1 x ¾in)

DMC stranded cotton
Cross stitch

■ 310		▨ 666	
⁄ 435		▨ 738	
✕ 604		＼ B5200	

Backstitch
— 310

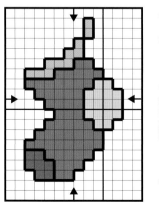

Christmas Stocking

Stitch count 16h x 10w
Design size 2.9 x 1.8cm (1⅛ x ¾in)

DMC stranded cotton
Cross stitch

■ 666		▨ 726	
▨ 704		▨ 995	

Backstitch
— 310

Stitching Materials and Techniques

This section describes the materials and equipment required and the basic techniques and stitches used. See pages 100–103 for Making and Finishing Cards and refer to Suppliers on page 104 for useful addresses.

Stitching Materials

Fabrics

The designs have been worked over one block of 14-count Aida fabric. You could work the designs over a 16-count or 18-count Aida but the finished size of the design will be smaller – see Calculating Design Size, right. You could also work the designs on a 28-count evenweave fabric instead, in which case stitch over two fabric threads.

There are patterned fabrics available, which can add an extra dimension to your stitching, as you can see on the baby cards on page 10.

Threads

The projects have been stitched with DMC stranded embroidery cotton (floss) but you could match the colours to other thread ranges – ask at your local needlework store. The six-stranded skeins can easily be split into separate strands. The project instructions tell you how many strands to use. DMC Light Effects threads have been used for some designs for a metallic shine, and DMC Desire memory thread on some cards for a 3D look.

Needles

Tapestry needles, available in different sizes, are used for cross stitch as they have a rounded point and do not snag fabric. If adding beads to your cross stitch designs you will need a beading needle, which is longer and thin enough to pass through the holes in seed beads.

Frames

It is a matter of personal preference as to whether you use an embroidery hoop or frame to keep your fabric taut while stitching. The designs in this book are all quite small so you might find it easier to work without a hoop or frame.

Stitching Techniques

Preparing the Fabric

Before starting work, check the design size given with each project and make sure that this is the size you require for your finished embroidery. Your fabric should be about 7.6–10.2cm (3–4in) larger all the way around than the finished size of the stitching, to allow for making up.

Finding the Fabric Centre

Marking the centre of the fabric is important regardless of which direction you work from, in order to stitch the design centrally on the fabric. To find the centre, fold the fabric in half horizontally and then vertically. The centre point is where the two fold lines meet. This point on the fabric should correspond to the centre point on the chart, which is indicated by arrows at the side of the chart (see illustration below).

Calculating Design Size

Each project gives the stitch count and finished design size but if you want to work the design on a different count fabric you will need to re-calculate the finished size. To do this, count the number of stitches in each direction on the chart and then divide these numbers by the fabric count number, e.g., 140 x 140 ÷ 14-count = a design size of 25.5 x 25.5cm (10 x 10in). When working on Aida, work over one block. Working on evenweave usually means working over two fabric threads, so divide the fabric count by two before you start calculating.

Using Charts and Keys

The charts in this book are easy to work from. Each square represents one stitch. Each coloured square, or coloured square with a symbol, represents a thread colour, with the code number given in the chart key. Many of the designs use three-quarter stitches to give more definition and some use half cross stitch, usually for areas of sky or background. Solid coloured lines show where backstitches or long stitches are to be worked. French knots are shown by coloured circles. Larger coloured circles with a dot indicate beads. Each complete chart has arrows at the side to show the centre point, which you could mark with a pencil.

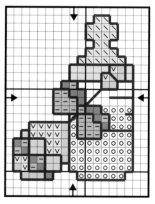

Starting and Finishing Stitching

Avoid using knots when starting and finishing as this will make your work uneven when mounted. Instead, bring the needle up at the start of the first stitch, leaving a 'tail'

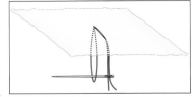

Fig 1 Starting to stitch

of about 2.5cm (1in) at the back. Secure this tail by working the first few stitches over it. Start new threads by first passing the needle through several stitches on the back of the work.

To finish off thread, pass the needle through several nearby stitches on the wrong side and cut the thread off, close to the fabric.

Washing and Ironing Work

If the fabric has become a little grubby after stitching, you can wash it. Most threads today are colourfast and should withstand hand washing in lukewarm water using a mild detergent. Avoid the use of lemon-fragranced detergents as some of these can react with metallic threads to discolour them. Once the embroidery is washed, rinse well and lay out flat to dry completely. Alternatively, you can use a cool iron to dry the embroidery by placing it right side down on a thick layer of towelling and pressing gently.

The Stitches

Backstitch

Backstitches are used to give definition to parts of a design and to outline areas. The charts may use different coloured backstitches. Follow the diagram, bringing the needle up at 1, down at 2, up again at 3, down at 4 and so on.

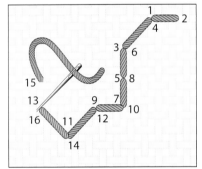

Fig 2 Backstitch

French Knot

French knots have been used as eye highlights and details in some of the designs. Use two strands of thread for the French knots in this book.

To work, follow the diagram, bringing the needle and thread up through the fabric at the exact place where the knot is to be positioned. Wrap the thread twice around the

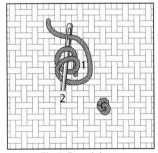

Fig 3 French knot

needle, holding the thread firmly close to the needle, then twist the needle back through the fabric as close as possible to where it first emerged. Holding the knot down carefully, pull the thread through to the back leaving the knot on the surface, securing it with one small stitch on the back.

Cross Stitch

A cross stitch can be worked singly (Fig 4a) or half cross stitches can be sewn in a line and completed on the return journey (Fig 4b).

To make a cross stitch over one block of Aida, bring the needle up through the fabric at the bottom left side of the stitch (number 1 on Fig 4a) and cross diagonally to the top right corner (2). Push the needle through the hole and bring up through at 3, crossing the fabric diagonally to finish the stitch at 4. To work the next stitch, come up through the bottom right corner of the first stitch and repeat the sequence.

To work a line of cross stitches, stitch the first part of the stitch as above and repeat these half cross stitches along the row. Complete the crosses on the way back. Note: for neat work, always finish the cross stitch with the top stitches lying in the same diagonal direction.

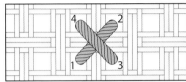

Fig 4a Cross stitch worked singly

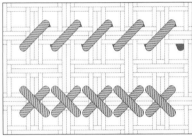

Fig 4b Cross stitch worked in two journeys

Three-quarter Cross Stitch

Three-quarter cross stitches give more detail to a design and can create the illusion of curves. They are shown by a triangle within a square on the charts. These stitches are easier on evenweave fabric than Aida. To work on Aida follow the diagram, first working a half cross stitch and then making a quarter stitch from the corner into the centre of the Aida square, piercing the fabric.

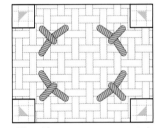

Fig 5 Three-quarter cross stitch

Half Cross Stitch

This is just what it says, a single diagonal line. Make sure all diagonals are facing in the same direction.

Attaching Beads

Sew beads on with half cross stitch, using sewing thread that matches the fabric and a beading needle or fine 'sharp' needle.

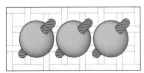

Fig 6 Attaching beads

Making and Finishing Cards

This section describes the basic tools and materials you need for card making. It is followed by instructions on how to mount finished work on single-fold and double-fold cards, how to make your own cards and how to finish off and embellish your cards. For those who want to design their own cards, see the useful tips on page 103.

Card-making Tools and Materials

General Tools

★ Pencils, a sharpener and eraser – for sketching designs and marking apertures.

★ Scoring tool or embossing tool and steel ruler – for marking and scoring folds on cards, for applying rub-on stickers and for dry embossing when applying a brass stencil pattern.

★ Eyelet setters and small hole punches – for attaching eyelets and brads to card and paper. Traditional tools include a hammer and setter; modern versions consist of springs or resemble sophisticated pliers.

★ Punches (not essential) – for cutting shapes from paper.

★ Stencils, stamps and ink pads.

Cutting Tools

★ Scissors – a general pair for cutting paper and a separate pair for cutting fabric.

★ Craft knife, cutting mat and steel ruler – for cutting card or paper when layering. The mats are self-healing and will protect work surfaces. Steel rulers (more durable than plastic) are also used for cutting apertures in double-fold cards.

★ Guillotine or paper trimmer – as an alternative to a craft knife, these are great for obtaining a straight edge quickly and accurately. Many have guide lines and a measuring grid and some have interchangeable blades which make wavy or perforated edges (ideal for RSVP invitations).

Materials

★ Ready-made single-fold and double-fold base cards – these can be bought in craft stores and a selection of different shapes and sizes is useful. See pages 101–102 for making your own cards.

★ Card stock – a good selection of card in different weights and colours will be needed, which can be used for layering or as base cards. Textured card is also available, including glitter, handmade and embossed.

★ Patterned or scrapbook paper – available in different sizes, textures and colours. It can be double-sided (the reverse having a different pattern) or have a white core revealed when torn (chamfered edge). Often acid-free (will not damage the fabric/stitching), it often forms the basis for layering and card making.

★ Embellishments – manufacturers often produce embellishments and toppers to coordinate with different ranges of paper and these can include buttons, ribbons, brads, eyelets and stickers, which are often self-adhesive. They can make the task of matching items quicker and easier. Other types of embellishment include beads, jewels, wire and charms. Embellishments don't have to be shop bought – leaves, shells and pressed flowers also provide perfect finishing touches.

Adhesives

Adhesives fall into two types, wet and dry, each with their own merits. Dry adhesives bond instantly, are quick to use, do not wet fabric and are invisible. Wet adhesives allow for repositioning and are good for layering paper or card together, where slight movement may be needed to get a perfect alignment. It does have a drying time (refer to each product individually), doesn't always have the strength that dry adhesive tape has and will often mark fabric.

★ Dry adhesives – these include double-sided tape, which is used to attach fabric to the underside of mounts on double-sided cards, for layering fabric on to card and for fixing embellishments in place. 3D foam sticky pads, which have dry adhesive on the top and bottom surfaces, are useful for decoupage and layering.

★ Wet glue – this includes paper glue sticks, which are used to stick paper to the front of base cards, and glitter glue, which is more decorative than functional.

Card-making Techniques

This section covers the card-making techniques needed to create the great cards in this book, including using single-fold and double-fold card mounts, layering elements together and adding embellishments as finishing touches.

The Stitcher's Birthday card shown right (charted on page 90) shows how effectively cross stitch can be combined with papercraft and card making techniques. Just two small cross stitch motifs teamed with some card, patterned paper and sewing embellishments create the perfect card for a sewing fanatic. After reading through this section, you will find it easy to use this card and the others in the book to inspire you to create your own fabulous card designs.

This sewing card shows how needlecraft and papercraft can be combined for stunning results. To finish this card, a strip of gingham patterned paper was stuck down the left side of a tall yellow base card. The fabric patches were layered on to coloured card and stuck to the base card. Themed embellishments were added, along with real buttons.

This 1st birthday card (see page 14) has pinking sheared edges and was mounted as a patch on a single-fold card.

Making a Single-fold Base Card

Shop-bought cards are convenient but it is so easy to make your own, which means you are not restricted to size and colour. It is a good idea to have a wide selection of card stock for this purpose.

1 Chose a medium-thickness card in a colour suitable to coordinate with the stitched design. Decide how big the finished size of the card will be – which may depend on how many layers you want to add and the finished size of the embroidery. Cut a piece of card twice this width, but the same height.

2 Use a ruler and scoring tool to measure and score a centre fold line. Following the crease, fold the card in half. It is now ready to decorate and then the embroidery can be mounted on to it.

Tip
Card is available in different weights and a medium-thickness card should be able to stand upright without bending or collapsing.

Using a Single-fold Base Card

Many of the cards in this book have been layered on to a single-fold base card. In order to do this the fabric must be prepared to prevent the edges from fraying (although sometimes you may want to fray the edges to give a more rustic appearance). The fabric can be prepared using one of two methods.

Using pinking shears Create a patterned edge with pinking shears by making a full-length cut and keeping the zigzag pattern aligned along the length.

Using iron-on interfacing This adhesive webbing is fused into place on the back of the stitching with a medium iron (or following the manufacturer's instructions), which stiffens the fabric. The edges are then trimmed using fabric scissors.

This stylish birthday card (see page 38) was backed with iron-on interfacing, with edges then cut neatly, and then mounted as a patch on a single-fold base card.

Using a Double-fold Base Card

Traditionally cross stitch cards are mounted in a double-fold card with an aperture cut in the centre panel, which acts like a mount to display the embroidery. A romantic card (right) has been mounted in a circular aperture mount.

To mount work in a double-fold card you will need: a ready-made card mount (aperture size to fit the embroidery) and craft glue or double-sided adhesive tape.

1 Trim the edges of the embroidery to fit into the card allowing at least 2.5cm (1in) each side to overlap the aperture. Apply a thin coat of glue or strip of double-sided tape around the inside of the card aperture. (Note: some cards already have this tape in place.) Peel off the backing tape.

2 Position the embroidery face up on the work surface. Hold the card with the sticky side facing the fabric and, checking that the stitching is central, press the card down firmly. Fold the spare flap inside, sticking in place with glue or tape, and leave to dry before closing.

This romantic love birds card (page 62) was mounted into a double-fold card with a circular aperture to complement the shape of the stitching.

mark the sheet of card into three equal sections

cut an aperture to fit the embroidery

score and fold

score and fold

trim 2mm (¹⁄₈in) from this edge

Fig 7 *Making a double-fold card*

Making a Double-fold Base Card

Making your own double-fold cards allows you to choose more colours and shapes. The size and shape of the aperture will depend on the size of the finished embroidery. Generally speaking, the right and left borders should be equal. When using a square base card, the aperture should have the same size border on all four sides. When using a rectangular base card the bottom border is often cut slightly wider than the top.

1 Start by taking a large piece of card (A4 for example), choosing a colour that complements the stitched design.

2 Place the card face down, use a ruler and pencil to measure and score two faint pencil lines, dividing the card into three equal sections. Gently score down the pencil line with a scoring or embossing tool and then fold.

3 Rub out the pencil lines and place the card face down on a cutting mat. Using a ruler and pencil draw the aperture on to the centre panel. Use a sharp craft knife and steel ruler to cut out the aperture making sure you keep the corners neat. Trim about 2mm (¹⁄₈in) from the left-hand side to allow the card to close more easily.

Decorating Base Cards

Many of the cards in the book have patterned paper stuck on to the front of the base card, which is a great way to emphasize the theme of the card and introduce further colour and even texture. This technique can be used on both single-fold and double-fold cards.

1 Apply glue to the front of the base card; in the case of a double-fold apply the glue to the central panel.

2 Place the patterned paper over the glue and press into place. Trim the paper edges so that they align with the edge of the card.

3 For a double-fold card you will also need to cut around the aperture. Place the card face down on a cutting mat and use a craft knife and steel ruler (if the aperture is square or rectangle), or a pair of scissors or craft knife (if the shape is oval or circular) to cut the paper following the shape of the aperture.

The Number 1 Brother card (page 42) has coloured and patterned paper covering the double-fold card, enhancing the racing theme. Football Mad (page 28) has birthday-themed patterned paper on the front of a single-fold card, with layering at an angle to create interest.

Using Layering

Layering is a really useful technique that allows you to add depth, interest and colour to your cards and create a professional look. Many different elements can be used including coloured card, patterned papers, ribbon and trims. When adding layers use a guillotine or paper trimmer if possible to give straight edges and to save time.

1 Start with the top layer of your embroidered fabric and use either double-sided tape or a glue stick to attach this on to a slightly larger card layer.

2 Cut each layer successively larger than the preceding one, with the smallest layer on top. In most cases layers should have equal borders on all four sides, however each layer can have a different size border to the layer beneath and this can add extra impact.

Tip
If you alternate layers between dark and light, the colours will stand out against each other and look more striking.

This Thanksgiving card (page 78) and Christmas card (page 82) show how effective layering can be.

The New Home card (page 66) shows how specialist memory thread can be shaped into simple embellishments. The Retirement card (page 66) illustrates how novelty buttons can be used.

Adding Embellishments

You will see from the embellishment features at the start of each chapter that embellishments and toppers are many and varied and can make a great difference to the look of the finished card. They are perfect for creating themed cards and bring added interest and a 3D look to a card (see above and left).

Generally, all 3D embellishments should be added to your card last, except brads and eyelets which should be added before the fabric is mounted within an aperture. Many of these decorations are self-adhesive or can be fixed in place with double-sided tape or craft glue.

Card Designing Tips

If you have been creatively stimulated to design your own cards, here are some useful tips to help you begin:

★ Decide first if the design is to be mounted in a double-fold aperture card or as a patch on a single-fold card.

★ Choose a colour scheme to reflect the theme of the card or the age of the recipient.

★ Stick to just a few colours as this will help unify the design – too many colours may make the finished card look too busy.

★ Play around with different layouts on a card to decide which looks best.

★ Use a notebook to make simple layout sketches.

★ Layer different elements to create interest and add colour and texture.

★ Before fixing embellishments in place on your card, move them around to find the most pleasing position and combination.

★ Generally speaking, adding embellishments should be the last step when finishing a card.

★ Don't go overboard with embellishments – they should enhance and complement your stitching, not overpower it.

Acknowledgments

Thank you to the following suppliers who have provided materials used in the cards in this book: DMC Creative World Ltd for threads and fabrics; Trimcraft for supplying Making Memories, Dovecraft and DCWV products; Vesutor for supplying Sandylion products; DoCrafts for Papermania products; CraftsULove and The Scrapbook Shop for general paper craft products. Thank you also to my team of expert stitchers: Michaela Learner, Fiona McIvor, Barbara Clarke, Lynne Beckett and Cathy Wines. Thanks too, to my project editor, Lin Clements.

Suppliers

Refer to the suppliers listed below for local stockists of products used in the book. Some manufacturers have online stores. Visit www.joannesanderson.com for further designs and stitching and papercraft advice.

Ali Craft (online shop)
www.ali-craft.co.uk

Bramwells (suppliers)
www.bramwellcrafts.co.uk
For Paper Adventures, Provo Craft and Rob & Bob Studios products

Craftime
www.craftime.com (for nearest store/stockist)

Crafts U Love (online shop)
Tel: 01293 776465
www.craftsulove.co.uk
For Making Memories, Doodlebug, Dovecraft and DCWV products

Crafty Bitz (suppliers)
www.craftybitz.co.uk (for nearest stockist)
For Crafty Bitz and Craft House products

DMC Creative World Ltd
Tel: 0116 275 4000
www.dmc.com

DoCrafts (suppliers)
www.docrafts.co.uk
For Papermania products

English Paper Company
PO Box 14401, Tamworth,
Staffs B77 9GB
Tel: 0870 122 4399
www.englishpapercompany.co.uk

Habico Ltd
Tong Road Industrial Estate,
Amberley Road, Leeds LS12 4BD
Tel: 0113 263 1500
www.habico.co.uk

HobbyCraft (super store)
Tel: 01452 424999
www.hobbycraft.co.uk (for nearest stockist)
For Artoz-Artwork, Craft for Occasions, Express Yourself D.I.Y and Paper Cellar products

Impex (suppliers)
Tel: 020 8900 0999
www.impexcreativecrafts.co.uk

MIC (online shop)
Tel: 01707 269999
www.miccraft.net

PaperCellar (online shop)
www.papercellar.com

Personal Impressions (supplier)
www.richstamp.co.uk
(for nearest stockist)
For K&Co products

The Scrapbook Shop (online shop)
Tel: 0191 3757515
www.scrapbookshop.co.uk

ScrapGenie (suppliers)
www.scrapgenie.co.uk
(for nearest stockist)
For Chatterbox, Doodlebug, MOD, Pebbles Inc and Prima products

Southfields Stationers
(online shop)
Tel: 0131 6544300
www.southfield-stationers.co.uk

Trimcraft (suppliers)
www.trimcraft.co.uk
For Making Memories, Dovecraft and DCWV products

Vesutor Ltd (suppliers)
Tel: 01403 784028
www.vesutor@aol.com
For Sandylion products

WhichCraft (online shop and UK store)
Tel: 01302 810608
www.whichcraftuk.co.uk
For Anna Griffin products

Willow Designs (online shop)
www.willowdesignstamps.com

About the Author

Joanne Sanderson has been designing cross stitch projects for many years and contributes to many popular needlecraft magazines. She also produces designs for DMC kits and publications. Her designs also appeared in *Magical Cross Stitch*, *Quick to Stitch Cross Stitch Cards*, *A Cross Stitcher's Countdown to Christmas* and *Cross Stitch Cuties* for David & Charles. Her papercrafting book, *3D Rubber Stamping*, was published in 2008. Joanne lives in South Yorkshire with her daughter.

Index